FOREWORD BY ROBERT HERJAVEC

# 9

AN OLYMPIC GYMNAST'S
INSPIRING STORY OF REINVENTION

## LIVES

## BY 35

# MARY SANDERS

DUNDURN
PRESS

This book is a memoir that reflects the author's present recollections of experiences over time. Some names and characteristics have been changed, some events have been compressed, and some dialogue has been recreated.

All images courtesy of the author unless otherwise noted.

Publisher: Kwame Scott Fraser | Acquiring editor: Julie Mannell | Editor: Olga Filina
Cover designer: Karen Alexiou
Cover image: Getty images/Jonathan Ferrey

**Library and Archives Canada Cataloguing in Publication**

Title: 9 lives by 35 : an olympic gymnast's inspiring story of reinvention / Mary Sanders ; foreword by Robert Herjavec.
Names: Sanders, Mary (Gymnast), author. | Herjavec, Robert, 1962- writer of foreword.
Identifiers: Canadiana (print) 20230201628 | Canadiana (ebook) 20230201717 | ISBN 9781459751552 (softcover) | ISBN 9781459751576 (EPUB) | ISBN 9781459751569 (PDF)
Subjects: LCSH: Sanders, Mary (Gymnast) | LCSH: Gymnasts—United States—Biography. | LCSH: Acrobats—United States—Biography. | LCGFT: Autobiographies.
Classification: LCC GV460.2.S26 A3 2023 | DDC 796.44092—dc23

We acknowledge the support of the Canada Council for the Arts and the Ontario Arts Council for our publishing program. We also acknowledge the financial support of the Government of Ontario, through the Ontario Book Publishing Tax Credit and Ontario Creates, and the Government of Canada.

Care has been taken to trace the ownership of copyright material used in this book. The author and the publisher welcome any information enabling them to rectify any references or credits in subsequent editions.

The publisher is not responsible for websites or their content unless they are owned by the publisher.

Printed and bound in Canada.

Dundurn Press
1382 Queen Street East
Toronto, Ontario, Canada M4L 1C9
dundurn.com, @dundurnpress 𝕏 f ⓘ

# 9 LIVES BY 35

*For my children, Ava and Gabriel: May you always follow your heart and achieve every dream imaginable. Mommy loves you unconditionally and believes that you can push through endless barriers that life may bring you, my angels.*

*For my husband and family: Thank you for supporting me through my many lives. I love you.*

*For my mother: You sacrificed everything for your children and gave me my Olympic dream. I would not be where I am without you. You are my real-life guardian angel, best friend, and a true gift from God.*

# CONTENTS

# FOREWORD

I've been an entrepreneur for most of my life, having started a number of small businesses with two employees and building them into global companies worth more than a billion dollars, all in the cyber security space. Currently, I run one such company called Cyderes, which is the end result of a company I started many years ago. But most people will recognize me more from my work on television, as a "shark" on *Shark Tank* and as a "dragon" on *Dragons' Den*. I'm also a bestselling author of three books, including *Driven: How to Succeed in Business and in Life* and *The Will to Win: Leading, Competing, Succeeding*. I was born in a Communist country and came to Canada as an immigrant on a boat. I have been a television producer, waiter, and collection clerk. I was married later in life for the second time. Suffice to say that I've lived many lives, which is one reason I can relate to Mary's memoir, *9 Lives by 35*.

Another reason is that I've had the honour of knowing her personally for the last 10 years!

From the first day I interviewed Mary to be my executive assistant, I knew there was something special about her and, that if given the right opportunity, she could flourish. Her background was unique to say the least. You don't often encounter Olympian and Cirque du Soleil acrobat on a resume, especially not in the corporate world. But I knew she was special, and I needed to take a chance on her. She was focused, accomplished, down-to-earth, and had a fire in her eyes. One of my first memories of Mary was after I introduced her to someone as a "former Olympian." She corrected me without missing a beat. "Olympian," she said. "Once an Olympian, always an Olympian." I knew right then and there Mary was a force to be reckoned with.

I often ask Mary, "Who are you?" because she is constantly reinventing herself, and I admire that about her. When she told me that she had written her memoir, I repeated the question because while the world was turned upside down during the pandemic, Mary gave birth to two children, worked full-time for me, and, with a newborn and a toddler at her feet, still found the time to write a book. She continues to surprise and impress me.

When I read *9 Lives by 35* and followed her on her journey to the Olympics, learning about her gruelling schedule on and off the stage and her many life path transitions, it all made sense to me why Mary is who she is. She's a strong, intelligent woman who has experienced so much, trained hard, travelled the world from a young age, and competed on the world's largest stages, all while dealing with pain, loss, trauma, and heartbreak. She's changed directions in life over and over, constantly reinventing, because she's had to. And as I can personally attest, whatever the pressure or spotlight, she remains calm and gets the job done. A skill that was no doubt honed during her years of training, competing, and performing.

It is because of her struggles to become the woman she is today, and how she's learned from those experiences, that I believe anyone reading her book will be able to take inspiration, courage, and strength from its pages. Mary's personal mantra of the three *R*s — reason, reinvention, and right — is the kind of takeaway that people of all ages, genders, and backgrounds can implement in their daily lives in order to achieve their goals.

When Mary asked me to write her foreword, I was honoured. One of the great privileges of my life is that it affords me the opportunity to meet some extraordinary people — such as Mary. She has been a constant in my life since we met, and is not only an employee, but also a friend who is like family to me. No matter what the future holds, I know Mary will continue to be in my life. I would like to say to all readers who have picked up this book and who are reading this note that *9 Lives by 35* is a true testament to the fact that in life anything is possible. Mary is living proof that the only way to achieve greatness is to work hard. I always say, and it's a line that Mary knows very well, that all life owes you is an opportunity. I'm proud to say that Mary continues to grasp those opportunities, and I can't wait to see what the next nine lives look like for her. I'll always be her biggest fan. And I think after reading her book, you will be, too.

Sincerely,
Robert Herjavec

# 1ST LIFE:

# CHILD GYMNAST

I sit cross-legged on the floor of the gymnastics gym watching girl after girl perform routines. Tumble, tumble, tumble, backflip, land, and present. They are ten, eleven, maybe twelve. Now it's my turn. I take my place. I breathe deep. Then I go! Run, run, dance, leap, cartwheel, but instead of another trick, I stagger to a standing position. Frozen on the floor. My routine forgotten. I look at the crowd of onlookers, but I see only one face. My father's. His expression is as motionless as my little body. He is embarrassed. I have humiliated him because he is a gymnastics coach and I am his daughter who just showed the judges, the gymnasts, the audience, that I'm not as good as the other girls he teaches. I am five years old.

I come off the mat and expect my father to give me the cold shoulder, turn his back on me, but he doesn't do either of those things. Instead, he crouches so he can look me in the eye, and says, "You go back out there, and you do it again. You know your routine." I do as I am told. Perhaps because I am the youngest, or maybe because the officials know or fear my father, I am given a second attempt. I return to the competition floor. This time I run, I cartwheel, and I continue my simple routine. I present to the judges. I am elated. I glance over to the crowd, searching for my father. I find him. I can't tell by his expression, but I think he is proud.

○

The memory of that day, one of my first gymnastic competitions, returned only after my Aunt Corinne reminded me of the incident. But it was a prime example of my father's coaching style, particularly when it came to me. I was expected to be as good as, or better than, the other young girls he trained because from an early age I was his "little Olympian." It was his goal that I make it to the top of the sport and represent my country, an ambition he didn't achieve for himself when he was a young gymnast. Over time, either through his sheer will, my urge to please, or osmosis, it became my goal, too. But the journey from the little girl who forgot her routine to a world-class athlete performing on the Olympic stage in Athens, and a life beyond, was full of dramatic twists and turns — losing a parent at eight, watching my single mom sacrifice, financial instability, moving constantly, bankruptcy, a failed marriage, a near-death accident, and so much more.

I like to say that I'd lived nine lives before I turned thirty-five, hence the title of this book. The proverb, "A cat has nine lives. For three he plays, for three he strays, and for the last three he stays," always stuck with me. And as my own multiple lives unfolded, the proverb became more poignant and personal, informing my life philosophy, what I call the three Rs: reason, reinvent, right. I'll explore how the three Rs played out in each of my nine lives, but I simply mean this: Reason: What is your reason? What makes you get out of bed every day and thrive? Reinvent: When one door closes, break down more doors! Thriving on the word "no." When one path does not fulfill your "reason" it is time to reinvent and get moving. Right: You have the right to choose your life. You have the right to say no and to stay on *your* path. You have the right to reinvent. I want to share all I've learned in the hope that my story can inspire anyone who has ever felt alone, or that they were the underdog, or that life was overwhelming, but who still dreams of achieving what might seem impossible. It is possible. I'm living proof. Here's what happened.

O

I was born on August 26, 1985, and christened Mary Jeanne Elizabeth Sanders. That same year *Back to the Future* was in theaters, and *Heaven* by Bryan Adams was on the airwaves. Live Aid had already happened. Brian Mulroney was prime minister of Canada; Ronald Reagan was president of the United States. The economy was on an upswing after slogging through a recession. And I was living with my family in Toronto. Judging by the photographic evidence, my family embraced the decade's fashion. Not that I knew a thing about the era's New Wave music, or teased hair, blue eye shadow, and shoulder pads. But by the time the 1990s hit and ushered in a completely different aesthetic, I got hooked on pop culture. I showed up on my first day of high school dressed as Cher from *Clueless*, which is now super embarrassing to think back on, but I thought it was what the cool girls were doing. But it was gymnastics, not fashion, movies, or music, that defined me and where my story, my "first life," that of a child gymnast, begins.

From day one I saw the world upside down. I mean that literally. From the moment I could walk, I climbed and hung — upside down and sideways — from all sorts of apparatus. I loved handstands, rolling, and tumbling, too. Whatever the move, I twisted and twirled and made it my own. My father noticed and it must be how his dream of my future Olympic glory was born.

You see, my father, Fred Bates Sanders Jr., was a three-time All-American Big Ten Champion in trampoline, which made gymnastics part of my DNA. He started his athletic career as a diver in high school, but switched to trampoline. It was those early years as a diver that made him emphasize form over difficulty in executing the tricks. By that I mean that he would not break form to accomplish a difficult trick he was trying to learn. It was a characteristic he carried with him onto the gymnastics floor and the trampoline, and later as a coach. My dad was an educated man, as well as an elite athlete. He received a bachelor's degree in physical education from the University of Michigan, and then he completed a master's degree in school administration at the University of North Carolina at Chapel Hill. He first taught at the UNC before making the move to Toronto, where he taught at the University of Toronto and coached at private gyms. His own stellar competition record, as well as his commitment to training other gymnasts, made him revered by his peers and he was eventually inducted into the Region 8 USA Gymnastics Hall of Fame. I have met many people who tell me what an impact he made on their gymnastics and personal careers.

If I got my gymnastics talent from my father, my hard-work ethic and "everything will be ok" attitude I owe to my mom, Jacilynne (Jaci) Ann Harvey. She was born in Toronto, and her father worked in the railway. They moved to Sarnia when she was young, and she took up tap dancing. She loved to dance. But when they moved back to Toronto, the lessons stopped. She never asked why or to take them again. Same when her parents were told what a talented swimmer she was. There was no mention of extra money for lessons or encouragement to pursue athletic excellence. My mother was of the generation where kids didn't ask. "Gimme, gimme never gets," my mom was told. This is the same era when people would tell a tearful child, "Don't cry or I'll give you something to cry about!" Is it any wonder my mother kept her feelings to herself throughout her life? Instead of talking about her feelings or focusing on them, she focused on achieving goals, and that she did, becoming something of an overachiever, earning a bachelor of science in nursing, and later, a master of education degree. She was career-oriented and worked hard throughout her twenties as a nurse in public health. Her athletic passion was marathon running, one she had to give up at the age of fifty-three following two knee replacements.

If there was one thing that has kept my mother at peace and able to cope throughout her life, it was, and still is, her faith. She is a devout Christian and believes that God will take care of her and her loved ones. She survived polio as a little girl, and when she was growing up, her mother would remind her always to be good, telling a young Jaci, "You must make it up to God. You must pay God back." More on faith and my family later, but suffice it to say that I am a product of both my parents. The showmanship and confidence in sport of my father, and the faith and perseverance of my mother.

My parents met in Toronto, by this point my father had left North Carolina and moved his first wife and their two kids to Canada to take a job coaching at a gym. When his first marriage fell apart, he got a job coaching at the University of Toronto, and began dating Corinne Harvey, my aunt. When Corinne ended things, Fred asked Jaci out. She got permission from her sister, and Jaci and Fred fell in love and got married. My mother was in her early thirties at this point and knew how to survive on her own. She had a good job, a career in fact, with salary and benefits. She wasn't looking for a rich husband to take care of her, that she could do on her own, thank you very much. So, the dashing Fred Sanders swept her off her feet with his charisma and charm. He was a former star athlete with a steady job at a top university, of course child support meant less for his new family, a fact that was never resented, though it meant my mother had to make up the shortfall.

But my father had his flaws. One was his selfish side. Perhaps it was the fact that he was a champion at a young age, with all the confidence and love of the spotlight that entails. This aspect of his personality came out in ways that impacted my mother and their marriage, although I was too young to be aware of these tensions. He loved to dress in stylish clothes, splurging on a fabulous coat, even if it meant less money to care for his family. If he had two hundred dollars from coaching, one hundred would go to my mother for food, the other one hundred for his beer. He loved to drink. Money was a source of friction. To hear my mother tell it, they didn't discuss budget or splurges, there were no calls asking if they could afford this or that. Take, for example, the story of the ceramic baby. My father just came home with it one day. It looked like one of those Royal Doulton figurines, and it cost some crazy amount. My mother wasn't impressed. On the one hand, it was sweet because it reminded him of us. On the other hand, he blew a month's worth of groceries for what was essentially a pricey knick-knack. I still have the ceramic baby, by the way. The other thing he loved was cactuses. He collected them and gave them to us. My brother Mike still has his to this day. My father might have been stern on the gymnastic floor, but he was a hell of a great dad at home.

Years later, I learned that toward the end of my father's life, my parents' marriage was disintegrating. My mother had written him a letter pleading with him to change. Fred had bought Jaci some jewellery, admitting to her that "I haven't been a great husband." But then he got sick. Had he lived, my mother wasn't clear what the future would have looked like.

But an unhappy marriage wasn't her only sacrifice. Jaci gave up everything (and I mean everything) for her children. To me she is a superwoman, and continues to be my idol. I owe everything to her;

nothing will ever amount or live up to how much I appreciate her. She is *the reason* I am who I am.

My parents gave me life, and also my brothers, Matthew and Michael. My parents had a thing about Christian names that start with *M*. I also have an older half-brother Mark (*M* again), and half-sister, Kelly (no idea how a *K* slipped into the family, but there you have it), from my father's first marriage. I'm the baby of the family. Of all of Fred's offspring, I was the only one with a desire to follow his footsteps into gymnastics. My siblings were all athletic, but they preferred other sports. It's a credit to my parents that they didn't push the other kids into a sport they didn't want to do. But I showed both an aptitude and an interest in gymnastics, and my father pushed me, and hard.

My family and I lived in Toronto until I was three years old. Then at some point that year, the family, along with our dog, an English Springer Spaniel named Freckles, picked up and moved to Salt Spring Island, British Columbia. Even in the late '80s, the small town of Salt Spring was considered completely off the map and very "hippie." Organic farms, artisanal crafts, you name it. It was a big move across the entire country, but my parents wanted to escape the city and live a simpler life. The main motivator for this move was my brother Matt. He had attention deficit disorder, and his doctor had suggested that a quieter environment, one with a lot of structure, would help him. That fact, coupled with my parents taking a trip to Mexico that made them question why they lived in the rat race of Toronto, ensured that we went westward.

While it was a culture shock for my parents and brothers, personally I don't remember much of Salt Spring Island other than our big blue house. There was something special, almost magical about it. That house was just beautiful in my eyes, and we loved it there for the few years we were blessed to live in it. As a young girl, it's funny the memories your brain retains. There was a loft, which was the scene of some pretty spectacular teddy bear fights between my brothers and me. The house also had a staircase where I sprained my ankle more than once running and playing, an injury that would come back to haunt me in my career. Our backyard connected to our neighbours' yard through a little path, and they had chickens. I would visit the hens daily to watch them play under the red heat lamps, and I'd help feed them and take care of them. I loved the country.

To support the family, my mother got a job as a personal care worker and my father opened a gym where he coached young gymnasts, and it was here that my official training began. At five I started doing ballet as many little girls do, but I'd head straight to my father's gym right after to train (or pretend to) with the big top-level girls. He was paid to coach other people's children, not his own, but I'd be there with him and try to learn by watching and trying to copy them. There wasn't a lot of coaching going on during these early days between my father and me. Yet the expectation was there, despite these other girls being ten or older, and they were much bigger (and seemed more talented) than me.

As time went on and he took more of a formal interest in my training, he became as hard on me at age five as he was on his top-level gymnasts. He pushed me to join the intermediate classes when I was barely as tall as the girls' hips. As the older girls would tumble with power and strength and do high-flying skills into the "pit," an area with lots of foam to cushion the landing, I was eagerly trying to pull off a cartwheel back walkover, never mind trying to achieve any air or height during my attempts. But my tricks were never as skilled as the older girls. And I would often see the look of disappointment in my father's eyes. "Why weren't you as good as those girls?" he'd say. Or "Look at those girls, you need to be able to do what they can do." I mean, I was half their age, but in his eyes, I was always behind. "When the going gets tough, the tough get going," was his favourite line. I always wanted to make my father proud of me. I knew he loved me, but I also knew he wanted me to be the best possible gymnast I could be.

Even as I got older, my father was tougher on me than his other pupils. I never looked for affirmation because he rarely gave it. Yet I wanted nothing more than his approval, his admiration was as necessary as air. I would feel sad if I wasn't good in the gym that day or wasn't able to do what he asked of me. I never felt good unless I made him proud. Just thinking back on that day when I forgot my routine is painful. But lesson learned, from that day forward I was overprepared, so I never forgot a step or trick again.

O

I'm standing a few feet from my father; he is talking to the father of one of the older girls. The other father winks at me. I smile. My father glances at me, he tells the other dad, "That's Mary. She's my little Olympian. One day she's going to be at the Games." I don't know exactly what this means because I am too young, but I hear pride in his voice when he talks about me. I will go to the Olympics because it will make my father happy.

I recall my father referring to me as his "little Olympian" on a few occasions, and to my face. He also called me other endearments, like "peanut," but "little Olympian" was the one that made me feel special. According to my mother, there was never a formal discussion, parent to parent, about me being Olympics bound. It seemed to be a secret between me and my dad. To my mother my gymnastics was a hobby. She would be the shoulder to cry on when I got frustrated or worried and say, "As long as you're happy and doing your best, that's all that matters." She never pushed me, but I know she saw something in me as well and didn't want me to quit. She never knew the pressure I put myself under to make Dad proud, or that what mattered most to me was to never complain and disappoint him. I learned from him that you don't deserve a pat on the back for every move you do.

What this all meant to my young mind was that by the age of seven I thought I had it all figured out. Gymnastics was more than a sport; it was a way of life and the *only* one I knew. I would train as hard as I could alongside my father, and one day, we would be at the Olympics together competing on the world's toughest stage. Then the worst thing in my young life happened.

My father was diagnosed with multiple myeloma, bone marrow cancer. Of course, I didn't know that at the time, I was far too young to understand even if my parents had tried to explain. Truthfully, I have little memory of what, if anything, was told to us. It's all a blur. But the feeling of that time has stuck with me. Without explanation things started to change. More and more, I was at home with only my mother and two older brothers for company. My father wasn't around much, or if he was, he didn't spend time with us as he once did. I was told simply that he was too sick to coach me. I stopped going to his gym and started taking gymnastics lessons in Victoria, on Vancouver Island, which was a ferry ride away. Mom and I did that three or four times a week. Eventually, the truth was shared: My father was sick and in the hospital. Multiple myeloma is a very aggressive cancer that affects the body's lymph nodes, so it spreads quickly and is very hard to detect. The prognosis wasn't good. But his illness impacted our family in a myriad of ways beyond his inability to coach me.

Without my father's income, my mother opened a bed and breakfast in our house to help pay the bills. Her job as a nurse simply wasn't enough to make ends meet. It must have been a scary and lonely time for her. And being on the opposite side of the country, far from any family or support network, made us isolated, too. Help did arrive in the form of Aunt Corinne, who travelled to Salt Spring to lend a hand. With three young children only three years apart, my mom certainly needed an extra pair of hands and eyes, and my aunt was like a second mother to us even then. It would turn out that Aunt Corinne would devote much of her life to help raise us in the absence of my father.

The bed and breakfast worked short-term, but eventually my father moved into that spare room because it was on the main level, and he became too weak to make it up the stairs. The loss of this extra income was a further blow to my parents and added stress to my mom.

However, despite it all we still tried to maintain some semblance of normalcy, including eating meals as a family. I remember us being so happy during that brief period, and it felt like life had returned to how it was before my father's illness. As young as my brothers and I were, we were able to be hopeful that life would, in fact, be normal again, our father would get better. I'd have my coach and daddy back. But one night during dinner, my father suddenly disappeared. I didn't notice he'd left the table. I got up and searched for him. I pushed open the bathroom door and there he was, asleep, sitting on the toilet, looking very sick. I tried to wake him, but he was snoring away. I knew something was very wrong at that moment, and the hopes of having my daddy back to normal were dashed.

On another night, days or even weeks later, I was too young to recall, an ambulance was called while we were safe in bed asleep. The sound of the vehicle, the door opening, the voices of the paramedics and my parents woke up all three of us. We watched my father be put on a stretcher to be taken to the hospital. But before he made it through the front door, he called for Matthew. With all of us around the stretcher, as if my father knew this would be the last time he saw his family, he told his son, "You are the man of the house now, Matthew, take care of your mother, sister, and brother." At the time we kids didn't really understand the weight of that statement, but I believe my brother has carried that heavy message with him throughout his life.

We didn't get a daily report from our mother as to how our father was doing in the hospital. I continued taking the ferry back and forth to gymnastics, my brothers went to swim practice, and my mom juggled work and caring for us with help from Corinne. Life went on as usual, except that my father wasn't home. My mother did such a good job keeping us so busy that we never thought twice about the worst possible outcome.

O

It's a sunny afternoon, we are seated around the kitchen table again, my brothers and I eat and joke and chatter away when the phone rings. I watch my mom cross the kitchen to answer it. Her voice is very quiet, but I can hear her talking and she is very polite to whoever is on the other end. Then she hangs up. But she doesn't come to us right away. She stands with her back to us with her head in her hands, not making a sound. I watch her. I know bad news is coming. Then she gathers herself, turns around, and asks us to join her on the small sofa behind the dining-room table. As we sit with our mother, she relays the most devastating information a child could ever hear. "Your father has passed away and has gone to be with God. He loved you all very much and will see you again in heaven." We all cry and hold one another.

The memory of that morning has stayed with me. But how I felt in the moment is a blur. My father was diagnosed in May of 1993 and passed away in October of the same year. It was very quick. I was eight, Michael was ten, and Matthew, eleven. We were all children, yet in that moment we all grew up, knowing that from that day forward our childhood would never be the same. My mother likes to say that even as a little girl I had wisdom and perception beyond my years. What I do recall from this period was trying not to cry. My father had instilled a tough-skinned attitude in me. I was a sensitive child, but he always tried to make sure I had thick skin to cope with judges during competitions, and I applied that to my life even at such a young age.

I don't remember much of the funeral other than my half-brother Mark from Toronto crying. I had never seen him cry before and I knew this was devastating for him. Mark had more memories of Dad than we did, he'd had more years with him. I wanted to be tough for him and not cry or be weak. I felt instinctively that this was probably the worst thing that would ever happen to me, and if I could numb myself and train myself not to cry when others did, I would be stronger than anyone and nothing could hurt me, ever. I think it was at that moment I learned how to compartmentalize my emotions. Definitely a coping mechanism. Looking back, I realize I probably learned some of this from watching my mother, too. She had been raised not to show emotion or dwell on feelings, to just move forward and get it done. No one asked her how she felt about things. And she didn't ask us. We just carried on. I've had to teach myself as an adult that feelings are positive and expressing them is healthy. But it's not easy for me, and I have to continually work on it.

"The Lord himself goes before you and will be with you; he will never leave you nor forsake you. Do not be afraid; do not be discouraged" (Deuteronomy 31:8).

O

I mentioned earlier that faith was vital to my mother's life. It became essential to mine also. She would hand-write Bible verses and leave them around the house for me and my brothers to find. The one above was typical of what she'd choose for us. Faith can be a touchy subject in our current cultural climate. But I am a person of faith, it is the reason I have been able to persevere through some of the toughest moments of my life.

Take the time I had a terrible flu. I'd never been so sick in my entire young life. Our living room had floor-to-ceiling windows, and as I lay limp and listless on the couch with a soaring temperature, my parents contemplated taking me to the hospital. I recall their chatter in the background as I was looking out the window and saw something, make that *someone*. This entity was childlike and hovering in the air. I stared at this apparition for what felt like hours as my fever was so high and I could barely move. The child wore kid's clothes and sneakers as they hovered in the clouds outside my house. At some point as I stared at this figure, I fell asleep. When I woke up, my fever had broken. I was able to move, felt much better, and wasn't weak or disoriented anymore. I looked out the window and the childlike figure was gone. My mother was so relieved and asked me what I was looking at out the window. To this day I believe it was my guardian angel.

Even when I did not feel like waking up early or on my only day off from training to go to church, I'm glad my mother made me. I always felt whole again afterward, and I've met lifelong friends through church. My family is Anglican, but we attended many different denominations of churches, Pentecostal and Lutheran to name two. I was never very close to school friends, but found a sense of belonging and purpose with my church friends. My life has been full of ups and downs, twists and turns, but my faith grounded me, and saying a prayer made any situation more bearable. I also see how it gives my mother peace and an ability to forgive even the worst behaviour in people. More on that later. Faith was just part of who we were as a family and stayed with us.

I remember as a teenager, travelling alone to a competition, opening my gym bag, and seeing my mother's familiar handwriting on a piece of paper. "Do not be anxious about anything, but in every situation, by prayer and petition, with thanksgiving, present your requests to God. And the peace of God, which transcends all

14

understanding, will guard your hearts and minds in Christ Jesus" (Philippians 4:6–7). Reading notes like these gave me comfort when I was lonely and gave me strength to train, but also let me know that even if I failed at this sport, if I never made the Olympics, my life would still be fine because God would take care of me.

I don't go to church every Sunday anymore and I'm not a Bible-preaching kind of person, but faith still gives me comfort. I pray to ask for forgiveness or when things get tough, I find prayer helps me cope in this crazy world. Even if you don't believe in God, I think believing in something greater than yourself is important. We are in control of our physicality, but I think it helps take the pressure off yourself knowing that there is a greater power that can help you through some of life's biggest challenges. And even as a child, my faith helped get me through my father's passing.

My father was buried at the Ganges Cemetery behind the church we used to attend every Sunday. (I went back years later and sadly, the church had turned into a movie theater, the cemetery was overgrown, and my father's grave was barely noticeable.) Even though my father wasn't a regular attendee at church, unlike my mom, my brothers, and me, he used to make beer bread for communion. (He sometimes used too much beer, but everyone loved it.) I think in his own way he was always spiritual, and I know he is in heaven watching over me every day.

My mom told me later that when she was at church the Sunday of my father's passing, the pastor abruptly stopped his sermon out of nowhere, and for some reason told the church that he had a calling to sing a specific song, "It Is Well with My Soul." He led the congregation in the song, it was so random, and no one knew why. My mom realized later that this was the exact moment my father had passed away in the hospital. I get chills every time I think about this or hear the song. It was my father's way of telling my mom that all was well with his soul and he was in heaven. My father wasn't a very religious man, but he did pray in his final hours and asked the Lord into his heart. I know that gave my mom a lot of peace.

After my father's funeral, my mother and I continued to ferry back and forth from Salt Spring to Victoria for gymnastics and my brothers stayed active, meeting new school friends and excelling at their sports. Aunt Corinne returned to help my mom, which made my brothers and I feel like we had two official mothers. It was fun. Like my mom, my aunt was an avid marathon runner, so sports and being active were always at the forefront in our home.

I remember one Christmas when my mom didn't have enough money for presents, she and Aunt Corinne made us teddy bears. They bought fluff to stuff the bears, sewing needles and thread, buttons, and fur, and made the best stuffed animals we ever had. We didn't know any better at the time, but they worked very hard to make these teddy bears so my brothers and I would have something to open on Christmas. We loved them and I still have mine. It was a lesson at an early age about being grateful for what I have, cherishing the small things, and pushing myself to work hard so I could one day provide for my family.

But it wasn't only financial struggles that caused stress in my mother's life. She also noticed I wasn't improving in gymnastics. It was like I was stuck, unable to advance up the levels. Taking the ferry back and forth a few times a week wasn't going to get me to the Olympics. She knew I had natural talent, but even the most naturally gifted athletes need proper coaching. Before I knew it, we were packing up. We sold the big blue house and boarded a plane back to Toronto. I wasn't the main reason for the move. She couldn't afford the house and felt the small-town life wasn't going to give us the opportunities that Toronto would. She wanted us to have big dreams and for her to have a better job and return closer to family.

O

Leaving Toronto at three years old and returning at nine was strange to say the least. City people were different, the schools were different, and it just felt busy, overwhelming, and confusing. I was a country girl in an urban centre, it didn't feel right, and I felt like an outsider.

We lived with Aunt Corinne in Scarborough for a while. She was a schoolteacher, and living with her gave us stability as we got accustomed to this big city–living thing. My brothers had no problem making friends at their schools, but I had a tougher time. For starters, I was a tomboy, my father used to cut my hair short. He would place a bowl on my head and cut around it. A "bowl cut" it was called. I looked more like my brothers than my beautiful mother. I was teased a lot in the beginning, but eventually grew my hair out and tried to conform and be "cool," but I was always just different. Honestly, we didn't have the money for me to look like the city kids. My clothes were mainly from Salvation Army or second-hand stores (my mom even made me some clothes) and as much as I tried, I just felt uncool.

Once we were settled, my mother asked around about the best gymnastics programs in Toronto, and we ended up at Seneca College. They assessed me and declared I was too low-level for my age and wasn't taught the basics properly. It was soon apparent that I'd fallen behind since my father's passing. We sought out a club that would accept me and we ended up at the East York Gymnastics Club. The owner, Sandi, greeted me with open arms and paired me with a coach named Vania, who took me in as if I were her own gymnast from the start. Vania's girls were disciplined, smart, and very good. I quickly learned that I needed to work very hard to catch up to their level.

Vania was from Bulgaria, had a thick accent, and was strict but had a very kind, loving heart. I felt safe with her and that I was where I needed to be. It was a good feeling after all the change we had experienced in the last year. I never thought I would feel the same way with another coach as I did with my father, but Vania's coaching style was the closest thing I'd experienced to him, and I respected her all the more for it.

Artistic gymnastics, which is the official name of the sport, where gymnasts perform routines on the bars, beam, floor, and vault, never came easy to me. I was tall, thin, not very muscular, and had very weak ankles (from spraining them on the stairs in the big blue house). The classic artistic gymnast is ideally short and muscular to have power to tumble and flip. Given that I wasn't built for the sport, I had to work very hard to catch up to the other girls in my level. Power wasn't my strength. I struggled on the floor (although I loved the dance and leaping parts) and vault, I was okay on the bars, but I excelled on the beam.

The funny thing is I was terrified of the beam and didn't like it at all, but it was my best event. I remember one day in practice, I was attempting a split leap and I fell and straddled the beam. That was traumatizing. Another time, I was attempting a front tuck and I landed with my face in my knees and gave myself a black eye. Another time, doing a back handspring, I missed my hand and cut my lip open and rocked a fat lip for a week. I still have a scar to show for it.

While these injuries hurt, they also helped me realize that I needed to be more confident in my skills, work harder, do more conditioning, and be stronger mentally. I worked very hard with the help of Vania, while still rocking that bowl haircut, and competed almost straightaway. It's common in the sport to throw you into competition as soon as you have a routine, even if an athlete is only ten, as I was. But despite my hard work, I placed almost last. It was the next year that I came into my own. Soon enough, I won five gold medals at the PAGC Rainbow Classic competition. It was a major milestone in my life, and I think it was for my mother as well. With all the sacrifices, taking those ferries back and forth in British Columbia, and making the move back to Toronto, was all worth it. This was validation that in a few short years I was at the top of the podium. I was very happy with myself, and I knew my father was looking down very proud of his "little Olympian."

While I had made progress, a long road lay ahead of me trying to advance to the national level. As a gymnast, as in most Olympic disciplines, you start out competing at the provincial level, then you can advance to the national level if you are top in your province. By the age of twelve, I had not perfected enough high-difficulty skills to advance to that level. And I continued to struggle with injuries. I had plantar fasciitis, which is also known as heel pain. Every time I would tumble or land a jump, it felt like a nail gun went off in my heel. It was excruciating. I also struggled with shoulder pain because my flexible ligaments couldn't hold my shoulders in their sockets while doing large skills like giants — when you hold onto the bar and go around and around in a circle with a straight body. So, despite my best efforts, I was falling behind again, stuck doing my provincial skills and unable to attain the new ones required to advance to nationals. And my flexibility and height just kept increasing. My gymnastics career felt doomed. All the sacrifices my mother had endured to get me to this level were for nothing. She continued to work endless jobs, drive me around to training and competitions, and pay for leotards, and I could barely complete a training session without tears of pain.

But I also felt as though I was disappointing my father. I would never forgive myself if I didn't go to the Olympics. I would wake up soaking with sweat after nightmares of bombing at competitions and not making the team. I knew I had something in me that was top level, Olympic level. I wanted to become an Olympian, but I could barely do a roundoff back tuck without pain and having to ice both heels. I felt like a failure. I was lost until Vania sat me down and told me she thought I should try rhythmic gymnastics. I had *never* heard of this sport. But it was about to change everything and would become what I call my "second life," the one that would lead me to the Olympics.

## What I Learned

**Reason:** My reason to get out of bed and thrive was first to make my father proud, then after he passed, to train hard to make the Olympics and honour his legacy.

**Reinvent:** But I had to accept that artistic gymnastics wasn't for me. I had to take a leap of faith, knowing God would protect me, and forge a new path as an athlete.

**Right:** Even though I was a young girl during this part of my life, I had a right to choose my path, which was gymnastics. I exercised this right, and the right to reinvent, so I could continue to have a reason to get out of bed and thrive.

O

Life One of a child gymnast was complete. Next up, Life Two …

# 2ND LIFE:

# RHYTHMIC GYMNAST

Quebec, 1995. It is my first competition as a newly minted rhythmic gymnast. I wear a hand-me-down leotard and start my ball routine. My goal is to jump in the air and throw the ball above my head while performing a split leap. Instead, I throw it too early and barely take flight, turning my split leap into a graceless leg-flailing jump, ending in a forward roll that resembles a flop on the floor. Yet miraculously, I catch the ball. It isn't pretty. I place almost last.

My humiliation doesn't end there. A day later I enter the gym and find the other girls watching a tape of the competition. They giggle at my routine. I'm a laughingstock among my peers. To cope, I make fun of myself to let them know I'm in on the joke. But I am distraught. As I stand and listen to their laughter, I think, *What am I even doing in this sport and what would my father think of me now?* I know he wouldn't approve. Yet I can't give up, I can't switch sports again. I need to see this through. I am determined and giving up is not in my DNA. I am ten years old.

O

For anyone who doesn't know what rhythmic gymnastics is, I often refer to it as "that Will Ferrell sport" because the actor comedically dances around with a ribbon in the movie *Old School*. My artistic coach Vania explained that because I was tall, very flexible, and had nice lines (which translated means good toe point and hyper-extended knees), she felt that I would excel in rhythmic.

Like artistic gymnastics, rhythmic was also an Olympic sport, but instead of performing high flying tricks, a rhythmic gymnast's tricks involved twirling ribbons, rolling balls, manipulating hoops, jumping through ropes, and juggling clubs, all performed without leaving the ground except for a split second during a jump or leap sequence, and all done on a very thin carpet without any springs or cushioning.

While I liked the sound of never having to pound the floor again or have a hard landing, I still didn't quite get it; plus, I could already see my father rolling in his grave. There was no way he would have ever allowed me to switch to rhythmic. Trading in the bars, beam, and floor for ribbon twirling and hula hooping — no way!

Vania knew a woman named Evelyn Koop, who was the owner of the Kalev Estienne Rhythmic Gymnastics Club, and she made an appointment for my mother to take me to watch rhythmic gymnasts in person. But even as a little kid, the feeling of failing my father weighed heavily on my shoulders. I didn't want to go. How was this even a sport? Artistic gymnastics was to be my ticket to the Olympics. I didn't think ribbon twirling would get me where I needed to be to make my dad proud, but I went to make Vania and my mother happy.

We pulled up to an industrial building and went down a few corridors until we finally came to Kalev's doors and opened them.

Inside, the lighting was dim, and it felt very dark and cold. I was used to lots of light, a necessity to see the bars or beam when flipping around. The next thing I noticed was that many of the girls looked like me — tall with a similar body shape — and they were all warming up in unison on a ballet bar. The last time I did ballet was when I was three years old, it wasn't part of an artistic gymnast's warm up.

I also noticed that the gym had two large carpets for training. Judging by the ages of the girls, one was for the younger gymnasts and one was for the older girls. As I was taking it all in, a very beautiful and serious-looking coach, who I had just seen stretching a girl in half, walked over to us. Her name was Svetlana. She introduced herself to my mother and smiled at me. She took a few steps back and looked me up and down, appraising me like a prize cow, but didn't seem impressed. We went to a mat, and she asked me to stretch and perform splits, bridge, over splits (which I hadn't done much of as an artistic gymnast), pirouette, and some leaps. She still didn't seem impressed. Yet, despite the scrutiny, Svetlana saw something in me that I didn't and agreed to take a chance on the little girl who had failed at artistic gymnastics.

All I felt was disappointment, confusion, and sadness. I had worked very hard in artistic gymnastics; it was my one and only love. How was I going to start an entirely different sport at ten and make the Olympics? It felt impossible. But as my father always said, "When the going gets tough, the tough get going." Never one to be left out, my mother would always add, "I can do all things through Christ who strengthens me."

The decision was made, and I left artistic gymnastics behind and began training in rhythmic. This wasn't an easy transition. Not only did I have to learn all new body techniques, I had to learn how to manipulate the apparatus. Twirling a five-metre ribbon without making it into a knot. Manipulating a hoop with straight arms for hours without letting my arms get tired. Performing split leaps through ropes. Rolling a ball from one hand to the other and balancing it between my head and back. Juggling clubs and not knocking my teeth out. All while getting stretched constantly by Svetlana and doing hours of ballet that was so foreign to me, while trying to be graceful with a smile. Easy, right?

While I loved my floor routine in artistic gymnastics because of the dance and expression of it, I didn't realize that rhythmic gymnasts performed with four out of the five apparatuses on the floor at every competition. I would have to learn four floor routines with different apparatuses, expressions, and music. While Svetlana was extremely patient with me, I felt like a goose in a lake of swans. I was surrounded by all these beautiful girls in leg warmers with matching leotards, their hair in tight beautiful buns, their faces perfectly made up, how would I ever evolve into that?

Despite my first competition disaster, I kept pushing forward and earned a silver medal at the 1995 individual all-around competition at the Provincial Championships in Level II. While I had earned gold medals before in the provincial category as an artistic gymnast, this felt like a huge achievement and a step in the right direction.

Remember those two carpets at the gym? There was the first, where I started to train with lots of girls around my age, coached by Svetlana. And then to our right, there was the other carpet, where the older girls trained. These older girls were flexible, talented, expressive, coordinated, and coached by one very scary lady named Lucy. She yelled constantly, threw equipment and CDs, and screamed in Bulgarian. Her choice of bleached blond hair, dark black eyeliner, red lipstick, and an all-black wardrobe only added to her intimidating persona. But I knew that if I wanted to make the Olympics I needed to get to *that* carpet. It was calling my name. I remember whenever Lucy would look over, I would show off and see if she noticed. She often didn't, but sometimes she would smirk at me. Eventually, my attempts worked, and I was invited to the big-girl carpet to begin a new journey. To be honest, I cried at first, because she was terrifying, but so was yet another big change in my young life.

Who were these older girls? They were Camille Martens, who became a 1996 Olympian, Emilie Livingston, who went on to compete at the 2000 Olympics, and Melissa Jung, who was a very successful National team member. I was about three to five years younger than they were, yet they were gracious and took me under their wings. They taught me to work hard (just like my father had instilled in me) and how to properly apply makeup (thanks, Melissa). Emilie graciously loaned me leotards to compete in because by this time they had become more extravagant and my mother couldn't afford them, especially because you needed four different ones.

As for scary Lucy, she had a fun and loving side to her. More importantly, she transformed me into a very expressive and unique rhythmic gymnast. Through Lucy I was able to improve my apparatus technique as well as learn from the other girls. From there my rhythmic career skyrocketed, helped by inspiration from the 1996 Olympic Games in Atlanta.

My father's brother, John, lived with his wife Peggy in Chicago. Every summer my aunt and uncle hosted one of us — me, Matthew, or Michael — at their home. It was my turn to visit during the Atlanta Olympics and I watched as much of the gymnastics competitions as possible. This was the year of the "Magnificent Seven," the gold medal–winning American women's artistic gymnastics team. These girls were my idols: Shannon Miller, Dominique Moceanu, Dominique Dawes, Kerri Strug, Amy Chow, Amanda Borden, and Jaycie Phelps. I'll never forget watching Strug stick her landing off the vault knowing she was injured. It was one of those athletic performances that was transformative, especially for an aspiring young Olympian like me.

Of course, I watched rhythmic gymnastics too, including our very own Camille, and was completely mesmerized and inspired. The sport's stars in Atlanta were Yana Batyrshina from Russia and Maria Petrova from Bulgaria. Yana was one of a kind. She had signature moves and was just gorgeous, the Audrey Hepburn of the sport. Maria was more serious and intense, and her routines expressed a deep emotion that you felt touched your soul. Maria was like the Meryl Streep of the sport.

Once I returned home, I tried to integrate elements of Yana's and Maria's routines into my own. I lived, ate, and breathed my dream. So much so that over the course of the next two years I nabbed the gold at the all-around eastern regionals in Novice Level IV, and then placed second all around at the National Championships. I also won at Elite Canada, which is a qualifier competition that can advance you to the nationals. For the first time in my life, I was named part of the junior national team, winning the national title in 1998 at the age of thirteen. It was the break I was looking for.

But all my hard work and success didn't mean life got easier for my family. By this point we also had a new father, my mom's second husband. According to my mother, it was my brother Matt, who was only twelve when we moved back to Toronto, who said, "Mom, I wish we could have another father." And that got my mom thinking she better start looking around for a father figure for the three of us. Enter Stan, who we would soon dub Stan the Man. She met him while ice-skating with her sister Corinne. Stan took my brothers tobogganing, took me to practice, and picked me up. He seemed like a fit, and a positive addition to the family. When she asked us what we thought about her and Stan getting married, we all said it was a good idea. We were kids, we just wanted our mother to be happy and to work less hard. Stan had told us all how financially secure he was. So, they were married with our blessing. We should have told her the truth; it would have saved us all some pain.

The marriage proved to be a disaster. Stan was a violent con man. He would pick me up at the gym in very short shorts with handcuffs hanging from his waist, as he told everyone he was a police officer. He wasn't. He would sometimes carry around a massive camcorder and say he worked undercover for the police and would film accidents or crimes and send the footage to the police to catch the bad guys. All of this was voluntary, not paid; he never wanted to actually put in the work at a real job. Instead, he lived off my mother.

He also didn't like to be wrong or be told what to do. Before my mom married him, he told her all sorts of lies about what a great career he had with lots of financial stability. My mom, being a good Christian with faith in humanity, and blinded by her determination to find that father figure for us, believed all his stories. He was a sixth-degree black belt in karate, he could break bricks with his hand (which my brothers often challenged him to do, and he would fail and then get outraged at them), a chef, a pilot, an undercover cop — you name it, "Stan the Man" was a master of everything (ultimately, as we discovered, he was a master at nothing).

Within a year their marriage unraveled in terrifying ways that included physical fights with my brothers. Once, I witnessed Stan throwing plates at Matt as he ran for his life. Matt, remembering our dying father's instructions that he was now "man of the house," was trying to stand up to this fraudster, but it was not a fair fight. Other times, I'd watch Stan grab my mother by the arm or throat and back her up against a wall.

Then one day, bravely, my mother kicked him out. Stan didn't take rejection well. He threatened to take her for everything she had, including the house. It was after he moved out that the harassment began. Phone calls, following my mother, that type of thing, but it escalated, culminating in my mother and me hiding under the sofa while her soon-to-be-ex was pounding on the door. We believed Stan was armed because he called my mother days before to tell her he was cleaning his gun. My mother and I were terrified at first, and then as the absurdity of the situation struck us, we began to giggle as we held hands while Stan the Man banged on the doors and windows. It must have been close to an hour we were under that sofa waiting for him to leave, praying he didn't break a window or force entry and find us. Lord knows what he would have done.

Eventually, he left and my mother called my half-brother Mark because he was a police officer at the time, and told him what had happened. Mark tracked down Stan, wherever he'd been staying, and told him in no uncertain terms to leave us alone. That the marriage was over, and it was time he moved on. It worked. We never heard from Stan the Man again. And he signed the divorce papers without trying to lay claim to any of my mother's meager savings.

There was one other aspect of Stan that made me even more grateful he was gone. I only told my mother this recently, but I felt very uncomfortable around him. For starters, he would tap my bum as I walked by, or lean in and talk to me inches from my face. Worst of all, at night he would sit on my bed and give me multiple long and open wet mouth (but no tongue) kisses. Never more than that, but enough to make me want to spend as little time possible with this man because I wasn't sure what he would do next. Of course, looking back on his behaviour as an adult, it was clear that Stan was abusive. But in the late 1990s, abuse wasn't on the radar like it is now; it wasn't talked about at every turn — there was no social media. I shudder when I think of him.

Suffice it to say, money was never a factor in my mother's relationships, neither with my father nor Stan. Her goal in life was to get married and have children. She never thought, *Does this person have enough money to support me?* Nor did she consider not dating a man because of his lack of money. She always felt her career would be enough. And she was right, in the beginning at least. Earlier in her nursing career, she did make good money, had her own car and apartment, shopped at Holt Renfrew, and was able to save. But as the years wore on, nurses' salaries were capped by the government and didn't keep pace with inflation. Toss in being a single mom to three kids, one with an expensive sport and big dreams, and it's a recipe for financial struggle.

It didn't help then that at the time, the Canadian Gymnastics Federation didn't have much of a budget for rhythmic gymnastics, because at this point our athletes didn't place on top of podiums in the sport. All costs for training, travel, leotards, you name it, came from the parents' pockets regardless of whether you were ranked number one in the country.

Despite these stresses, being named National Junior Champion was a big deal, and I began to travel the world to compete on the international stage. While I was excited about the results I was finally achieving, I knew that travelling was really expensive, costing money my mother just didn't have. To help offset the bills, all ninety pounds of me helped my brothers shovel snow and rake leaves to give my mom whatever scraps we were paid. When I travelled, instead of buying a drink from a vending machine, I would go to the ice machine and eat the ice chips instead. I suffered many sore throats as a result.

I was training alongside Emilie Livingston who, as I mentioned, was Canada's hopeful for the 2000 Olympics. Emilie and I embarked on many journeys together with Lucy. We would room together. We would sneak out to get chocolate bars if we could. And we would take a lot of trains between European cities. Back then there wasn't a designated smoking section, and Emilie and I would hold our breaths if we could, but we always felt like we were suffocating in the smoke and couldn't wait to get off those trains. Lucy was a smoker, so of course it didn't bother her. Also, at these train stations there weren't any escalators or elevators, so off we went lugging our suitcases that weighed more than our own body weight up and down the stairs. Lucy would wait at the bottom, holding only her designer purse, and wait for us to return to her to climb the hundreds of stairs again to carry her luggage up. Travel days were considered "days off," although half the time they were more exhausting than an actual training day.

Emilie and I competed at the Coupe d'Opale in Calais, France, together a few years in a row. Emilie was always very successful there. She spoke French, since her mother was from France, so it was amazing to see her on what seemed to be home turf even though she was born and raised in Canada. She translated everything for me, which I appreciated. Emilie was named "Miss Coupe d'Opale" because she was such an elegant rhythmic gymnast. I placed silver overall and competed in all four finals: one gold, one silver, and two bronze medals. The Calais newspaper said that "one of the best surprises was the Canadian Mary Sanders." Lucy was very proud. I had transformed from a pigeon-toed late bloomer to a junior champion and earned a name for myself on the international stage.

Soon after that I competed at the World Youth Games in Moscow against seventy-five of the best junior rhythmic gymnasts in the world. I placed twenty-eighth overall in Moscow but qualified for finals in hoop and placed sixth. I remember not wanting to compete in the finals. I just wanted to be done with that competition. It was intimidating competing on that level. There were such phenomenal rhythmic gymnasts that had been born into the sport and had a lot more experience than I did. We returned home and our gym congratulated us for all our success. I felt quite proud of myself that I was able to pull through at an international competition.

And here's a confession I will share with you now: I never liked competing. While I loved the performance aspect of the sport, I didn't like the nerves prior to stepping onto that carpet. I didn't like the possibility of failure and how that would affect my family and coaches. If I made even the smallest mistake, I would be extremely hard on myself. My mom knew how I felt and would send me Bible verses such as "Be bold and strong, for the Lord your God is with you" to help me get through the pressure. However, I did love the feeling afterward of all the hard work paying off and standing on the podium with gold medals around my neck.

By this point, back home we lived in a house in Scarborough. We had a pool and a trampoline in our backyard. My mom made sure that no matter how hard times were, she would remortgage the house to give us everything to make our childhood the best it could be. I would invite all my rhythmic friends and we would pretend to be the Spice Girls. I was Posh, because of course I was! We knew every move and every lyric of their songs. We were sisters inside and outside of the gym. To this day, some of my strongest relationships are with those girls. It's tough to describe that bond to the outside world. These were girls I travelled the world with, spent four to six hours per day, six days a week with, throughout my entire adolescent life. We ate, slept, and breathed rhythmic gymnastics. If we weren't training, we were at someone's house watching rhythmic. It was a lifestyle, and it still is. I can spot a rhythmic gymnast a mile away, even if I don't know them from my career, because there is an inexplicable bond.

I was grateful to have that bond in the gym, because I didn't have it anywhere else, especially not in school. I was always the odd one out. I was tall and skinny, my hair wasn't streaked like the rest of the girls, I didn't feel pretty, and I missed half my classes because I was travelling abroad competing. I couldn't hang out after school because I had to go to practice. I felt a disconnect from everyone because I was constantly thinking of the routines I had to do in the evening and how tired I was all the time. I remember wanting to put my head on my desk and just sleep. My eyes would burn watching the teacher write on the chalkboard. I could barely make out what they were writing because my eyes were just so heavy and blurry despite my twenty-twenty vision.

I remember once, I didn't have enough time to study for a French exam. These were oral exams performed out in the hallway and not in front of the entire class. When it was my turn, I told my teacher to fail me because I had no idea what the exam was about, and I had not prepared as I had just returned from a competition in Europe. To my shock the teacher was sympathetic, and asked me to perform whatever my coolest skill was right then and there, and he'd pass me. Surprised and relieved, I performed an illusion. An illusion is a very popular skill in rhythmic gymnastics. It's basically a flip without leaving the ground. Sure enough, I received a pass. If only all my teachers were this forgiving.

At the gym Lucy continued to intimidate me. She would make jabs at me and belittle me. She instilled the feeling of "you are nothing without me" every day so I would never forget that she was the reason for my success. She would yell at me if I made any error or wasn't expressive enough for her. I would deal with the yelling by rolling my eyes back and singing "Jingle Bells" over and over in my head to detach and not cry in front of her. We were not allowed to show weakness or cry and were expected to take the criticism. Sometimes it was constructive and other times it just felt mean and unfair. My teeth were crooked, and I remember her always making fun of my smile, to the point I would only smile with my mouth closed.

At fourteen I won the 1999 Ontario Junior Championships but then decided I needed a change. I knew my father wouldn't approve, but he wasn't here anymore, and I wasn't happy. I told my mom I wanted to quit. I wanted out.

○

If I had declared my gymnastic career was over while my father was alive, he would have put his foot down and insisted I carry on. But my mom never pressured me to stay in the sport. Her strong faith meant she knew that God had a plan for me. I was determined to find a sport that suited my skills, my natural gifts. I'd work hard and achieve Olympic glory in this as-yet-undetermined athletic endeavour. But what sport would give me everything that I'd given up? It made sense to my young mind that synchronized swimming, with its choreographed solo and group routines, would be similar enough to rhythmic for me to feel right at home. My dad had been a diver too, so in some way I would still be connected to a sport of his choice. My mom supported this new direction and set out to find the best club in the city. Swimsuits were bought, classes paid for, but as it turned out, synchronized swimming was not part of God's plan. I felt like a fish out of water, though technically I was in the water! I froze half the time and couldn't hold my breath at all. I was also negatively buoyant, which meant that I sank, and floating was not in the cards. So, although the synchronized swimming coaches appreciated my flexibility and physical lines, they also agreed that perhaps it wasn't the right direction for me.

Discouraged, I decided that maybe the Olympics wasn't the dream. Or at least, I could put it on ice while I tried another form of physical activity. I landed on ballet. Even though I never liked ballet, I was always good at it and had some experience. Perhaps if I worked at it as hard as I had at gymnastics, I might learn to love it. Goodbye Olympic gold, hello National Ballet of Canada!

My mom, ever the trooper who wanted to see her daughter achieve whatever dream she wanted, again searched for the best classes, and bought me pointe shoes. They were so painful, my toes bled, and I struggled to stay on them with my weak ankles. I was

33

slow picking up the combinations and my turnout wasn't very good, but I excelled in the aspects that required flexibility. I managed to get accepted to Canada's National Ballet School, but after deep consideration and discussion with my mother, I declined. I couldn't force something that just wasn't my calling. While I respected ballet and the difficulty of the art, it wasn't my strength, and I didn't want to start from square one all over again.

Throughout this period of turmoil, my mother and her unerring faith in God were like a beacon in the fog. Our Christian belief helped me put the pieces together. My mother instilled in me the certainty that the Olympics weren't God, rhythmic gymnasts weren't God. Only God was God. And I had to believe that he had a plan for me, I just had to listen. And as I mentioned before, I did, and do, have faith. And where faith led me was back to the rhythmic gymnastics carpet. This time, I made a pledge to myself that I would see it through to the end, praying and wishing that the end of the rainbow was made from the Olympic rings.

Naively, I thought I could literally walk in the door these few months later and pick up my apparatuses and everything would return to normal. Boy, was I wrong. I had gained weight, the equipment seemed foreign, the girls had inside jokes that I knew nothing about. I felt alone. Lucy, ever the diplomat, told my mom I had to go on a diet. This was the first time in my life that my weight was an issue. My mom and I used to go to Dairy Queen at the top of our street sometimes, but those trips stopped suddenly. It was a sad time and I felt I was being punished for taking time off to learn that rhythmic was the sport I was meant to do.

I did my best to regain my previous fitness level, and while still fourteen years old, I competed at the 1999 Nationals and placed second. But I was disappointed in myself because I believed if I hadn't left the sport for that brief time, then I would have had the gold medal. But I learned a tough lesson that year. If I was to ever achieve my Olympic goal, I needed to work harder, be better, and not let my mind overpower me with negative thoughts. The mind is a powerful thing. I would let it speak bad thoughts, frighten me, and tempt me into doing things that weren't necessarily right for me. I still struggled with Lucy and was frightened of her. But I and the other girls on Lucy's team continued training and went on to travel to many global competitions.

During this time Lucy arranged for some of her students to spend time at a training camp in her native Bulgaria at Neshka Robeva's training facility, which was legendary. Bulgaria was a hotbed for gymnasts; remember, my 1996 Olympic idol Maria Petrova was Bulgarian. So I, for one, was psyched. We ate, slept, and trained all under one roof. It was not one of those gorgeous historic European buildings; it had more of that Cold War vibe that felt like a jail with bars on the dorm room windows. I will say, despite the Eastern bloc atmosphere, or perhaps because of it, you did improve; you also lost weight because you weren't juggling school or other distractions.

One weekend, Lucy took us out to a house that her family owned in the mountains. There was nothing to do there. We were a bunch of tall, skinny, rhythmic girls in the wilderness, completely out of our element. It sounds like the plot of a bad horror film. We slept in the attic on small beds and played cards, did each other's hair, went for walks, and took turns playing on our friend's video game console. Technology wasn't as advanced or ubiquitous in the late '90s, so to have anything that required a battery was a big deal. One of the other girls, Kelly, and I would watch the only movie on VHS they had in the house, *Meet Joe Black* with Brad Pitt, on repeat. It was a beautiful movie. Thank God it was three hours long, because it took up most of our evenings.

Each night Lucy would cook up a feast with her family, while we sat up in our rooms waiting to be invited down to join them, but the invite never came. We would get watermelon and the scraps from the feast. If you think this sounds neglectful at best, and abusive at worst, you're not wrong. But hey, at least we didn't have to watch our waistlines! This type of treatment was common in the sport; especially in that era and with European trainers, gymnasts were often neglected while a coach lived it up with friends and family. In hindsight these European "camps" were an excuse for the coaches to see their families while our parents paid their way.

Of course, young girls can only take so much. And one night, Kelly and I were so hungry we snuck downstairs after the adults had gone to bed to scavenge for food. We opened the fridge to find a dozen pig's feet staring at us straight in the face. We shrieked and almost woke up the entire house. I did say "bad horror film," remember? The discovery was made all the more horrifying because Kelly was a vegetarian. Now too grossed out to eat, Kelly grabbed a water bottle from inside the fridge to take her vitamins. She threw five to ten pills in her mouth, opened the water bottle, and chugged. Within seconds her eyes started to water, her face turned red, and she didn't know whether to swallow or spit. She eventually swallowed but her mouth and throat were burning. We went to the tap to rinse out her mouth, but it kept burning. I began to get worried, so I grabbed the water bottle and took a tiny sip to taste it. It was vodka! We burst out laughing. I couldn't believe she had drunk almost half the bottle trying to put back her vitamins. She quickly felt dizzy, let's call it "drunk," and I helped her back upstairs and to bed. The next morning she had quite the hangover. We went to practice, and she was falling all over the place because she was still dizzy. Lucy asked her what was wrong. Kelly didn't answer right away, then she looked at me and we both started laughing. Despite our fear that she would be furious with us for sneaking downstairs so late at night, we eventually told Lucy the truth, but surprisingly she fell to the floor laughing hysterically. She gave Kelly the rest of the day off to recover.

The following year, after I turned fifteen, I moved up to the senior level and finished in third place, which was decent for my first year as a senior. My peer, Emilie, was number one in Canada and competed at the 2000 Olympics in Sydney. Her hard work paid off. She had done it; she was an Olympian forever. Her achievement was fuel for me. If she could do it, I knew I could do it. I was so proud of her.

O

By this point I was a freshman in high school. Money had become too tight at the Scarborough house with the pool and trampoline, so we moved to a townhouse in Ajax, which is a town east of Toronto. I had braces, streaked blond hair, and was starting to feel like a woman, although I was underdeveloped compared to a lot of girls at my school because of the intense training. Gymnastics sometimes causes your body to delay puberty, which was the case for me. However, I began to have a friend group and started to get noticed by boys. For the first time in my life, I felt like a "somebody" at school.

Despite living in Ajax, I went to high school at York Mills Collegiate Institute in Toronto, and the school was mostly accepting of my athletic career. They allowed me to skip gym class and take that class as a spare to complete my homework. The last thing I needed was more exercise and I used every minute of that spare class, so I had less to do in the evenings. But academically, it was hit-and-miss depending on the teacher. While there were teachers like the French teacher, who passed me once I performed a trick in the hall, there were some who barely passed me or didn't want me to graduate because I had missed close to 50 percent of my classes.

There was an English teacher who simply did not like me and did not support my gymnastic career. It was clear she took offense at me missing her classes and was intentionally failing me. I asked my brother Matt, who was an A student in English at university at the time, to write part of my paper to prove to my mom it wasn't me. I was correct; despite the quality paper, the teacher still flunked me. I was falling victim to some form of bullying, and I felt helpless. I think by the end of the year my mother had a talk with her or the principal, and I passed by the skin of my teeth. Funny how writing is now one of my favourite things to do. It brings me peace and clarity. Thankfully, I was very good at band and played the flute. I received a 98 percent grade, which allowed me to achieve an 80 percent overall average. This allowed me to graduate with honours and helped the school turn a blind eye to my lack of attendance.

But for me high school was never going to be what I saw on television. I couldn't go to parties or do the normal things that teenagers do because I had to rush to practice right after school. My friends would often try to convince me to "just this once" skip training and come to a party. I caved once, but that wasn't who I was. I was determined to be the best rhythmic gymnast I could be. Even the temptations of friends, boys, and parties couldn't distract me from that. It was tempting, and I had my moments, but I thank God every day that I had the strength to keep my eye on the prize: the Olympics.

Keeping my focus meant a gruelling routine for me and my mom. My typical morning would entail waking up at 5 a.m., getting dressed, and running straight into the car. I went to school in the city because that was where I trained while my brothers went to school near our house in Ajax. I would eat my breakfast in the car, brush my hair, and apply my makeup, all while my mom was navigating bumpy roads and dark streets because it was so early. Our car often smelled like spoiled milk because I would eat cereal in it and the milk would splash everywhere. The drive to the city was about forty-five minutes on a good day with no traffic. My mom would then drop me off at a friend's house where I would take a power nap on her couch until she was ready to go. My friend and I would then take the subway to north Toronto, which took another forty-five minutes, and then take a bus to school to arrive before the bell rang at 9 a.m. After school I would take another bus to a subway station, where a mother of one of the gymnasts would graciously pick me up and drive me to training, which was from four to eight, sometimes eight-thirty, every night. The same mother would take me back to the subway or her house, depending on how late my mother worked, and we would drive back home to eat dinner (depending on how my weight was that week). I would attempt to do my homework and get some sleep, hopefully before midnight. The next day, I would wake up at 5 a.m. and do it all over again. This went on for several years. It was exhausting.

I must give credit to my brother Michael because he would stay up late and help me with my homework time and time again. He was a natural genius at math, science, sports, and basically everything. I struggled in school. I struggled to be engaged and lacked interest. I didn't understand how learning about history, politics, math, and science would help me be a better athlete. But Michael was so patient with me and did his best to show me why these subjects were important, and he helped me complete my homework. I do have to disclose that perhaps he did a little more than just help me at times. If I had a strict deadline on a project, he would work with me to complete it. I just didn't have the strength sometimes to complete my projects or study for my exams. Michael always helped me make my deadlines.

Saturdays were tough because after the gruelling week routine with little sleep and juggling school and training, I would have a morning practice from nine to two in the afternoon. My only day off was Sunday. I loved Sundays more than anything, although instead of letting me sleep in, my mother would make sure I got up (granted, it was a slightly later wake-up call) to go to church as a family. I would often fall asleep, but my mom felt it was important for us to make time for God, and we needed to be there in person. I wanted nothing more than to sleep. I met some great friends at church who I really enjoyed spending time with because it helped me forget about gymnastics, even if just for a little while. They helped me see there was more to life than just competing.

And here I want to talk about my faith again, because it was a major factor in my ability to cope. Through my mom's guidance, regular churchgoing, and my own prayers, I was able to find comfort when I was sad or lonely. Faith gave me the strength to push through pain, tough coaching, unfair competition results, and exhaustion, all because I believed I was on the path that God intended for me. And if for some reason things didn't go my way, that was okay, too. Everything was all going to be all right for me and my family.

Just when things seemed to be returning to some form of normalcy for me and my athletic career, we switched gymnastics clubs. I was too young to be told the full story, but we understood that there was some drama and tension between Lucy and Evelyn Koop. We left Kalev and began training at Ritmika Rhythmic Gymnastics Club in Toronto. Annely Riga was the owner, and she became like a second mother to me. I would take breaks from training, sneak off, and go sit and talk with her. I would even sneak a candy from the candy jar in her office. Annely would often extend the monthly fees because my mom couldn't make ends meet. She was very gracious and played a vital role in my success. We were getting used to our new training facility when the unimaginable happened. Lucy disappeared from the gym. She would eventually, and mysteriously to me, be banned from coaching in Canada and leave the country. We never saw her again and had to move on with another coach.

How was I to continue without her? She was all I knew. In some weird way, I loved her very much. I knew she was the reason I had achieved so much success so quickly. She was tougher on me than my father ever was, but I knew it made me a better gymnast, even if her methods were wrong in some people's eyes. I feared I would not make the Olympics without her. I learned later in life that all these obstacles early on truly strengthened who I am and moulded me into the woman I am today. We pushed forward and were blessed to have a lady named Mimi take over as head coach, a woman who would take me all the way.

## What I Learned

**Reason:** My reason to get out of bed and thrive remained developing myself into an Olympic-calibre athlete. But beyond that I needed to support my mother in any way I could.

**Reinvent:** The transition from an artistic gymnast as a child — my first life — to a rhythmic gymnast — my second life — was a tough one. Especially at such a young age. But having the courage and the faith to make such a leap helped me, and it proved to be the right choice. We too often let fear of the unknown, or lack of confidence, stand in our way to make big changes. You have to let go of those fears. And if God isn't your version of faith, find what is, and lean into that faith in yourself.

**Right:** I had a right to quit gymnastics and explore other sports and art forms. My mother felt the same and gave me the independence to make such choices. And I also had the right to decide that quitting was a mistake, and to rectify that error by returning to rhythmic gymnastics. Never lose sight of the fact that you have a right to fail, to quit and try new things, and a right to admit mistakes and make amends.

O

Life Two as a rythmic gymnast was ready for the next level, Life Three ...

# 3RD LIFE:

# OLYMPIAN

August 25, 2004. One day before my nineteenth birthday. Finally, it is my turn. My first routine is the ball apparatus. Not my strongest, but a consistent one. As I warm up, my nerves start to overpower me. It is early and I am alone on a big warm-up carpet. They come to get me as I am up next. They walk me down many hallways until I come to an opening, and I hear the loud voices of the crowd on the other side of the curtain. I hold my ball tight, rub my hands back and forth on my towel because my palms are so sweaty. I blow on my hands and dry them off over and over. Then the curtain opens, I hear my name, and I walk out for my Olympic debut.

O

That moment is etched on my brain and will be until my dying day. But let's go back three years to 2001 and another moment of transition for me. Lucy was out. My new coach, Mimi, was in. She was an impressive person and was fluent in English,

Bulgarian, Russian, Japanese, and maybe even a few other languages I wasn't aware of. Aside from also being Bulgarian, Mimi was the polar opposite of Lucy. For starters, she was nice, which was a relief. And she was successful. She had been instrumental in bringing Japanese rhythmic gymnastics to the forefront. But her achievements as a coach came primarily from the rhythmic group competition, or so we were told. An enormous challenge lay ahead for Mimi and me. She had inherited multiple national-level individual gymnasts overnight. Needless to say, it was a major adjustment for all of us.

Where the challenge landed hardest was in creating my routines. It soon became apparent that when it came to choreography, Lucy had a knack for it, and Mimi did not. Don't get me wrong, she knew what worked and what didn't for the judges. But in terms of building an artistic routine from scratch, it fell squarely on my sixteen-year-old shoulders. I had to take creative risks without the safety net of having a skilled choreographer by my side.

I began searching for music and researching moves that the eastern European girls were doing to create a routine on my own. As I developed these routines, Mimi would offer opinions on the athletic side, leaving the creative choices to me. It was a lot initially, and I felt that pressure. If I messed up and my routine wasn't going to score, it would be my fault.

Yet, despite my initial anxiety, I soon discovered I loved choreography — and more importantly, I was good at it. As the other girls saw my routines and my competition results, they began asking me for help with their choreographies. The coach switch proved to be the freedom I needed to develop, not only as a rhythmic gymnast, but also as an artist and performer. And with my creative juices flowing freely rather than being under Lucy's controlling eye, I was able to truly customize my routines to match my strengths. And the results? Mimi guided me to two Senior Canadian Championship titles in 2001 and 2002. It was an incredible start to the lead-up to the 2004 Olympic Games.

During this period Mimi started to get on me about my weight. As I already mentioned, I had entered puberty late due to my training regime. This came at the same time as my braces came off and I started to look "pretty" to boys. I quickly learned that I liked the attention. High school brought me a circle of friends, which I'd never had before. These "normal" friends ate whatever they wanted, and I started to do the same. It showed. But at this point I didn't have much success in losing the added pounds, which frustrated Mimi.

It's no secret that weight is a big issue in sports of all types, but this is particularly true in gymnastics. There is actually a reason for the weight obsession that goes beyond aesthetics. According to studies, low body weight and low fat mass, when coupled with strength and power, are considered advantageous for the tricks we do in our routines, because this increases the power-to-weight-ratio. In other words the lighter and stronger we are, the higher we can jump, twist, and spin. A 2022 study noted that this dynamic "is critical for optimal gymnastics performance since athletes must rapidly transfer their body mass across space while overcoming gravitational resistance."[1] Sounds impressive when put that way, doesn't it? This constant struggle to be thin but powerful often leads gymnasts to diet hop, starve, or develop other unhealthy eating habits. The same study found "a higher prevalence of eating disorder symptoms in international compared to recreational-level rhythmic gymnasts." I believe it because I lived it.

From choosing not to eat past 3 p.m., to consuming ice chips for snacks, I worked hard at staying thin. But not as hard as other girls.

---

1 Ioanna Kontele, Tonia Vassilakou, and Olyvia Donti, "Weight Pressures and Eating Disorder Symptoms among Adolescent Female Gymnasts of Different Performance Levels in Greece," *Children (Basel)* 9, no.2 (February 2022): 254, doi.org/10.3390/children9020254.

My cohort had its share of eating disorders. We had to; it was simply a sacrifice one made to get to the top of the sport. But we didn't talk about it. And I didn't give it much thought other than that I resented forgoing the standard teenage fare my friends indulged in. Controlling what you ate was the price you paid for Olympic glory.

I continued to train hard and competed at the 2001 World Games in Akita, Japan, where I placed tenth all around, and at the World Championships in Madrid, where I finished twentieth all around. Yet, by far my best accomplishment during this period was winning the gold at the Four Continents Gymnastics Championships in Curitiba, Brazil. Being crowned champion was incredible, but there was another reason why this particular event was so special for me — my mom was in the audience. She never travelled with me because it was too expensive, but this was a big competition and one of the other mothers convinced her to splurge on a ticket. It was a proud moment for me to step out onto the competition carpet knowing my mother was finally able to watch me on the international floor. I was my mom's biggest fan, and it felt amazing that she was there cheering me on as my biggest fan.

Winning the Four Continents Gymnastics Championships gave me the title of the best rhythmic gymnast in all the western hemisphere. I was very proud of that title. I still have the trophy in my office to remind me of that day. However, even with the all-around win, I made one small error in the event finals. This is a round of competitions the next day that won't affect your all-around score or medal, but it gives you a chance to medal in individual events. I ended up with two gold, one silver, and one fourth place for my error with the rope. In my mind it wasn't a big deal, I had already won the all-around and that's what counted, but in Mimi's eyes I needed to be perfect. An impossible expectation. After the rope incident, for the remainder of the competition, she froze me out and flatly refused to speak to me or coach me during warm-up for the remainder of the event.

I was a very consistent gymnast who rarely made mistakes, so it felt unfair that I was such a disgrace in Mimi's eyes for making one error in eight routines. In a stroke of good fortune, my first coach, Svetlana, was there coaching another athlete, and she saw how Mimi was behaving and stepped up to help me. Svetlana was the one who had taken me on when I was the kid with the pigeon toes, and she started my career in rhythmic, so it was a full-circle moment for me.

O

Spring 2002, and the Athens Olympics were only two years away. It was crunch time for me as an athlete. But back home it was time for our family to move once again because we could no longer afford to own a house. We returned to downtown Toronto and my brothers, mother, and I moved into a three-bedroom apartment on a busy urban street. It was the only apartment my mom could afford that would allow three teenagers and our dog, Freckles, who we had throughout my childhood and teenage life. He was the fourth sibling of our little family and was our best friend.

Of all the homes we lived in, I loved that apartment the most. At first, I shared a bedroom with my mother, while my brothers got their own. It made sense because I wasn't home much other than to sleep. Eventually, being the selfless and generous person that she is, my mom gave me the bedroom so that each of her children had their own room and privacy. She slept on the couch with Freckles.

I still feel bad about that, even today. I should have let her sleep in my room in a comfy bed rather than on a couch full of dust and covered with animal hair. One day she woke up and her entire face was swollen because she had an allergic reaction to the animal hair on the sofa. It was awful, but she wanted to make sure we all had our space even if it made her sick. My brothers were graduating high school and getting all sorts of amazing university acceptance letters, and they both ended up attending the University of Toronto. They were excited about the next stage in their lives as I kept my focus on Athens. But money was still a major hurdle and I had to get creative.

For many people the word "fundraiser" conjures images of black-tie galas, endless champagne, bland meals of rubber chicken, and silent auctions. But for me and my fellow Toronto-based rhythmic gymnasts in need of funds for our team, it meant getting creative. We would perform for money. That sounds worse than it was. A group of up to ten of us, between eleven and eighteen years old, would find an outdoor space where lots of the public would see us and we'd do our gymnastic "tricks" for tips. Think of it as gymnastic busking and you get the idea.

I don't recall exactly whose idea it was, but we figured out that Torontonians liked to drink. In Ontario liquor sales are controlled by the provincial government through the Liquor Control Board of Ontario (LCBO). The LCBO runs a slew of stores that sell wine, beer, and all forms of hard liquor. Some of these stores are located in upscale neighbourhoods, so it was decided that "busking" outside an LCBO store would provide the most bang for our buck, or flip, as the case may be.

We would arrive in shifts and spend an entire day outside the store with a bucket as our tip jar. We'd dazzle the patrons with moves such as lifting our legs above our heads, cartwheels, walk-overs, and the big move was the "illusion" that had scored me a passing grade in French earlier. Basically, we were crazy, young, flexy girls traumatizing the buyers into giving us money. Which they did. We'd end up with a decent haul, from three hundred to over a thousand dollars on a good day.

The LCBO routines were a blast and really bonded us as a team, but it underscored how much money was actually necessary to stay competitive. In 1996 Sport Canada cut its funding to rhythmic gymnastics to zero. There was no other choice; if you wanted to keep a competitive edge in the rhythmic world, your parents were expected to pay for training, travel (including overseas) to competitions, and even leotards. It got pricey really fast. Affordability was an issue for some more than others, and I needed financial aid big time. My mom was struggling to support her three children and was stretched to the limit, forced to cut corners and sacrifice things she might need so that I could train and compete. This led to her filing for bankruptcy at one point. This added burden weighed on me throughout my training. It was stressful for my mother, who I felt needed a break from worry, I would do anything to ease the pressure on her. Performing tricks outside a liquor store was the least I could do.

The next competition was the 2002 Pacific Alliance Championships in British Columbia. I was looking forward to returning to the West Coast where I had spent a small part of my childhood on Salt Spring Island. It was excitement tinged with grief, because the last time I was in B.C. was when my father passed away. As the memories flooded back, it helped to motivate me more than ever.

Life is never without obstacles. So it was that during the training days I contracted a norovirus. A few athletes had been stricken with it and it spread like wildfire throughout the competition. A norovirus infection results in illness twenty to forty-eight hours after exposure, and symptoms last from twelve to forty-eight hours. I had "luckily" contracted it two days prior to competition day, otherwise there was no way I could have competed if I were sick on day one of competition. I lost about ten pounds in two days. Mimi and the other coaches were very happy because I looked even fitter, and my leotards were looser.

Somehow, I mustered whatever last ounces of strength I had and was able to hit the mat by the grace of God. I couldn't even practise in the warm-up area before heading to the competition carpet.

Instead, I lay on my back with a cold towel on my head watching the room spin. I was afraid to drink water. While I could handle the nausea, there was no way I could prevent throwing up on the competition floor and needed an empty stomach, leaving me extremely dehydrated. I took a few deep breaths and stepped out onto the gymnastics carpet and completed all my routines. Flawlessly. I won five gold medals, including the all-around and all-apparatus finals. I even beat out the favourite from the United States, who was much more experienced than me. It was a massive accomplishment.

With the awards ceremonies complete and five gold medals around my neck, I headed back to the hotel to rest and to try to eat something. I shared a room with one of my teammates from Toronto. She was younger than me, and we met the first day I entered Kalev's gym, as she was also one of Svetlana's students. She was already winning competitions, and she was a favourite in the sport before I even knew what rhythmic was. We were like sisters. Her parents would drive me to practice, and I'd sleep over at their house countless times. But when she entered the senior division, she would always finish behind me, including at this competition, where she made the podium but not the gold. Granted, she was two years younger than me, but she had been in the sport of rhythmic gymnastics many more years than me. This change in dynamic thrust our friendship into a rivalry, yet we were still close. Both of us were summoned by Mimi to go to her hotel room immediately. All I could think was, *What more could she possibly want from me?* I was weak, exhausted, dehydrated, and had given it my all and won the championships. I headed to her room feeling helpless and afraid of what came next.

I knocked on her door and she opened it and welcomed me in with a big smile. I was instantly relieved that I wasn't in trouble. And I quickly noticed she wasn't alone. In the room with Mimi were members of the USA Gymnastics Rhythmic Program, Jan

Exner (now Heise), the head of the program, and the team's head coach, Efrosina Angelova. I was confused. But I sat down and for the next hour listened as the American contingent spoke to us about the history of the U.S. rhythmic program, how they weren't entirely sure they had a chance to qualify the U.S. for a spot at the next Olympics because their current top athlete was injured and unlikely to be in shape for the 2004 Games. I had just finished ahead of her, and typically only one rhythmic gymnast represents North America in each Olympics.

The Americans had done their research. Both of us were dual citizens of the U.S. and Canada. Then they started on me specifically. They recited all of the achievements my father had accomplished as a U.S. gymnast. They also knew about my mother's financial struggles and expressed their admiration about how she did her best to send me to every international competition, but no one was sure how much longer she could afford to do so. Then they got to the point.

"Our athlete is injured, and we aren't sure if she'll be able to compete at this level again. Why don't you girls come and join the American team and we'll make sure you get to Athens in 2004?"

I was in complete shock. It was a fact that on the gymnastics circuit, the Americans had money and paid for everything for their athletes. And this was what they were offering us. In that moment I wanted to say yes. This was an opportunity to make my father proud and follow in his footsteps by competing for the U.S. and also to lift the financial burden from my mother. Maybe we could afford a place where she could sleep in a bedroom of her own again. We were told to think about it.

I went home and spoke with my mother. With the Olympics two years away, there were a lot more national competitions, Grand Prixes, and international world cups to compete in. Those LCBO fundraising afternoons were fun but not enough for me to reach

Athens. It was not sustainable, especially at the level where I was, and I wasn't getting the financial support from the Canadian Gymnastics Federation I needed.

Following years of disappointing finishes at prior Olympics, where no Canadians ended up in the top ten, the Canadian Gymnastics Federation had implemented a new rule that if you weren't the top in the world, they wouldn't send you to the Olympics. So essentially, if you weren't a medal contender, regardless of whether you had earned your spot and had rightfully qualified for the Olympics, you wouldn't be allowed to go and represent Canada. I didn't learn of this rule until 2002. At the time I was ranked twentieth or so in the world, but I was the top rhythmic gymnast in the western hemisphere, so rightfully I should have been invited to compete at the Olympics, but the Canadian federation saw things differently.

Out of respect I decided to speak directly to the Canadian Rhythmic Gymnastics Federation (the organization didn't formally join with Gymnastics Canada until April 2004) before making a final decision. After all, I was a Canadian and Canada was my home, where I'd grown up and trained so hard and overcome so much. I wasn't going to simply walk away without discussing it. But as anticipated, they had little to say. They didn't offer to help with any costs for training or equipment. Nothing. Their reaction amounted to, "That's nice, dear."

My mother was completely supportive of whatever decision I made. But for me, there was only one right choice. I accepted the USA Gymnastics offer. My teammate did not. Her family didn't need the financial help as much as I did, and they felt that switching countries wasn't the right decision for her. I went on to represent the U.S. from that day forward and never looked back. I had my entire family to think about, not just myself. I wasn't going to allow my mother to file for bankruptcy again. It was my turn to support my family and give back after years of sacrifices.

During this period I still had to compete at the Canadian Championships to keep my status. The 2002 Canadian Championships were just a few weeks after the Pacific Alliance. I took home the gold, making me a two-time Canadian Champion. Four months later, I competed at the U.S. Championships and took home the gold there as well. Here I was, a champion of two countries in the same year. Once they finished the paperwork, I officially switched countries and started representing the U.S. on the international level.

I was so happy, and nothing ever felt more right in my life. Everything I had accomplished, all the struggles and sacrifices, led me to this moment. Being supported by an entire nation and following in my father's footsteps leading up to the Olympics was exactly where I was meant to be. The president of USA Gymnastics at the time, Bob Colarossi, knew my father, and he would tell me lots of stories about him, many I'd never heard before. Bob also had an uncanny resemblance to my father which, in some way, gave me comfort, almost as if my father were, in fact, with me in some shape or form. Bob would also introduce me to people who knew my father as a coach or competed with him. They would tell me story after story, and I was just mesmerized. It was like a secret time capsule had been opened and this whole entire world existed about my father that I'd known nothing about. If I hadn't made the move, I never would have known so many things about him. On the practical side, I was now receiving athlete funding that would pay for my training, leotards, travel, hotel accommodations, and more. My mother finally had weight lifted from her shoulders. For me, however, the dark side of my decision was about to come to light.

I returned to Canada following my win at the U.S. Nationals on a high. While the club owner, Annely, greeted me with open arms and a big congratulatory bouquet, there was coldness from most of my fellow teammates. The majority of them didn't seem happy for me at all. But it wasn't until I took a closer look at our team photos that hung on the walls and bulletin boards in the lobby and hallways that I understood the depth of their negative feelings. My face had been disfigured in every photo. There were *X*s and thumbtacks in the middle of my face, in others my face was completely scratched out. I was deeply hurt. No one seemed to be able to look me in the eyes. I didn't know who had done it, or if it was a unified decision, but I felt as though I had been demonized for making a very difficult decision to better my family's future and for following a dream set out for me long before my father's passing. I didn't feel anyone understood the driving force behind my decision to switch countries. I was labelled a traitor from that day forward.

Even the mainstream press picked up the story. Canada's national newspaper, the *Globe and Mail* published an article that said, "[Sanders] was Canada's prize, a Canadian champion, the best Canada had." It then quoted Jean-Paul Caron, the president of Gymnastics Canada at the time: "We have given the United States a nice little gift."

The same story also included some hard numbers. "But the Olympics would have long remained only a dream for her if she had stayed in Canada ... Only in the past two or three years has Sport Canada reinvested in the federation, but it amounts to only $50,000 a year."

Ultimately, the story made my case and included a quote from me. "I definitely wouldn't be where I am today without [Gymnastics Canada] ... It's a shame that this new standard had to turn out like this."[2]

---

2 Beverley Smith, "Sanders becomes Canada's gift to the U.S.," the *Globe and Mail*, July 20, 2004. theglobeandmail.com/sports/sanders-becomes-canadas-gift-to-the-us/article1001339/

But by then I'd moved past the anger and hurt against my former Canadian teammates and was ready and proud to wear the red, white, and blue. People still ask me how I felt about such a monumental change. The truth is I felt no guilt about it. Canada couldn't support me in my goal, and my poor mother was at the end of her ability to do the heavy financial lifting. There was no choice. I am a proud Canadian, and a proud American. You can be both. But I had to choose, and I made the right decision for me. No regrets.

Besides, I didn't have time to dwell on the opinions of others. I needed to own my decision and focus on the road leading up to the Games. The people behind the U.S. rhythmic program were sympathetic about the difficulties I faced back home with feeling like a traitor in my own gym, so they uprooted me and allowed me train at the Olympic Training Center in Lake Placid, New York, with Efrosina, the U.S. national team coach, while Mimi remained in Toronto. I would travel back and forth to continue working with Mimi as well. She was dividing her coaching time between me and my teammates, who would all climb in the Canadian ranks, with me now competing for the U.S. I appreciated the change of training venue since I needed the focus. I felt at peace there, and that I was not alone. Everyone was in the same place as me, giving it their all to qualify and compete at the 2004 Olympics in Athens, the home of the first Olympic Games.

I loved the Lake Placid Olympic Training Center. I met all kinds of athletes from different sports. There was a cafeteria where we all ate. I was able to maintain a healthy diet while maintaining my weight. Physiotherapy was accessible multiple times per day. By this time I was battling turf toe. This is an injury most found among football players. I had aggressively stubbed my toe at practice one day and it had never healed. I could only go halfway up on my toes. I needed constant therapy for it, otherwise scar tissue would form and I wouldn't be able to move my big toe. I never broke any bones, thankfully, but this injury was a lingering nuisance. I also struggled with back pain, and would sometimes have a rib go out of place. I was very flexible but lacked muscle mass.

During this new training schedule, my routines, style, and health were in peak condition and my hard work was paying off. I went on to finish in the top fifteen at the Bulgarian Julieta Shishmanova Cup, Corbeil-Essonnes Grand Prix, Berlin Grand Prix, and Vitry Cup, and to win the gold at the Levski Cup in Sofia, Bulgaria. I also won five gold medals at the Pan American Games in Santo Domingo, Dominican Republic. Becoming a Pan American Champion was one of the biggest accomplishments of my career.

My turf toe was very severe at the Pan Am Games, and USA Gymnastics enlisted renowned sports doctor Larry Nassar to help get me through the competition. Of course, this was decades before the truth would come out and Dr. Nassar would become an infamous convicted sex abuser who would bring scandal to the sport. Thankfully, when he treated me on this occasion there was nothing amiss. That would happen later. During this era we gymnasts felt "blessed" to be in his presence, and he had a way of making you feel special. Of course, no one spoke the truth back then, that the way he had of making some girls feel "special" amounted to sexual assault.

As the year progressed, I had my highest finish and made history as the top ranked North American at the 2003 World Championships in Budapest. I finished eighth in the qualification all-around, seventh in the hoop and ball finals, and ended up tenth for the all-around finals. It was a long and gruelling competition because I had never qualified for the World Championship finals before. I made history, qualified the U.S. a spot in rhythmic gymnastics at the next Olympics and was on my way. The buzz was out that the new Mary Sanders was in town and was on a mission!

I had also won my second U.S. National title and was named Athlete of the Year. By this point I had graduated from high school and was able to go into my final year leading up to the Olympics with full focus on my training. I had also been accepted to Western University in London, Ontario. It would be my chance to be a "normal" student after I retired from gymnastics. At least, that was the plan.

I think many athletes would agree that the final year leading up to the Olympics is the toughest. While qualifying and earning that spot is hard, the final year you are exhausted, beaten down, and are still expected to continue improving and peak at the right time. Oh, and not get injured. There's a lot of pressure. My mother continued to slip Bible verses into my gym bag when I went away, such as "Be strong and courageous. Do not be afraid; do not be discouraged, for the Lord your God will be with you wherever you go" (Joshua 1:9); or "I can do all things through him who gives me strength" (Philippians 4:13). They helped a lot. As I keep saying, faith has always sustained me throughout the most challenging parts of my life.

However, the brutal truth was that the pressure did get to me. I struggled to remain mentally stable and went into many competitions without a sound mind, though I never sought help or was diagnosed. But I was isolated, lonely, depressed, and felt this constant push for perfection would never end. I was at my end physically and emotionally. I was starving most of the time to maintain a weight that was well below the average weight for someone my height, and I was beaten down from constant criticism at every practice. Oh, and pushing through injury and pain eight hours a day during training. I ran on fumes day in and day out. Never feeling like anything or anyone could help me.

When you're at the top of your sport and at the peak of your career, it can be a very lonely place. One that not many can understand, relate to, or help you with. I started to distance myself from my family, including my mother, because I was often overseas and didn't have a cellphone and didn't want to break down. I turned away from friends because I didn't have the energy to lie and tell people I was okay and hear how fun their lives were. Nor did I have the energy to comfort them and be "on" outside of the competition mat.

I knew going into many competitions that I wasn't going to perform well, but I didn't have a choice. I needed to put on a pretty face, smile, and go out there regardless. The struggle between your mental health and physical health is always a fine line. In order to compete well, it's important to be at peace and confident both mentally and physically. One cannot succeed without the other. However, the mental health of athletes wasn't at the forefront of priorities during my career, although thankfully that's changing. But for athletes of my generation, being mentally drained, expressing emotion like crying or frustration, showed weakness and would only make your coach more upset, so you learned to bottle everything up and suffer in silence.

Keeping my emotions in check also came naturally to me because that's how my mother was raised. She didn't get overly emotional, or dwell on her feelings, and I suppose from her I learned the same. Add in my father's tough love coaching style, which was reinforced by coaches like Svetlana, Lucy, and finally Mimi, and I was a gold medalist at not expressing emotion!

Another part of the run-up to the Olympic Games was drug testing. I was drug tested at least twice a month in my last few years of competing. I think I was drug tested even more when I switched to compete for the U.S. Somehow, I felt picked on, as I'm pretty sure no other rhythmic gymnast was drug tested as much as me. It felt like there was a target on my back ever since I switched countries, and many were waiting for me to slip up. The United States

Anti-Doping Agency (USADA) and World Anti-Doping Agency (WADA) came knocking on the door of the little apartment my family and I lived in. Most times the knock would come on my one day off before we left for church.

Regardless of the pressure, 2004 was my year to show the world that I could be a gymnastics legend like my father, I could defy all odds and change sports late in life and change the country I represented, all to achieve Olympian status.

During this year my family moved yet again, this time from downtown Toronto to the city of Mississauga after my mother became involved with a man who would become her third husband. I'll call him "Rick," and they had met online with Christian Mingle. Rick was a churchy, Bible-preaching kind of guy, the sort who was always in your face with the word of God and walked around with a Bible under his arm wherever he went, but we figured he was better than her previous husband, Stan. Of course, we were skeptical after all my mother had gone through last time, but she deserved love and happiness, so as long as she was happy, we supported her.

My mom and Rick began their relationship during this final training year, which meant I was barely around and didn't really get to know him or spend time with him. Suffice it to say I couldn't get a true reading of the type of person he was. My brothers, who were older than me, were also home less and less. And soon enough, my mother and Rick's relationship got serious very quickly, and suddenly all my belongings were in Rick's house that he shared with his stepson, Christian.

Mississauga felt foreign to me. I wasn't around for the move, and I came home from competition one day to a new neighbourhood, townhouse, and bedroom. Granted, it was a beautiful bedroom with all my medals and trophies displayed. I was lucky I had my brothers to do the heavy lifting and move everything for me, although they likely considered me a princess because of it.

Strangest of all was having to witness this elderly man I barely knew walk around in his boxers. Rick acted like one happy family a little too soon for me. I always had this feeling something was off, and I prayed he wouldn't "screw over" my mom as badly as Stan had. I was so busy and stressed with my gymnastics that I brushed my gut feeling about Rick under the rug. I really couldn't take anything else on my shoulders at the time, and my mom seemed happy (even though it didn't take much to make her happy). It turned out my gut was right — more on that later. I'm not sure which man was worse in the end, "Stan the Man" or Rick, but I'll let you be the judge. They were both abusive and hurtful in very different ways.

One thing missing was our dog Freckles. He had passed away while I was at the World Championships, but my family didn't want to tell me as they knew it would be upsetting and cause a distraction. He was part of our family and will never be forgotten. He was my friend at times when I felt I didn't have any. You know the saying "Dogs are a man's best friend," well, Freckles was indeed my best friend and would lie with me when I would cry myself to sleep if I had a bad training day, or if I was feeling bullied or alone.

I spent a lot of 2004 alone. I would train sometimes in Toronto, sometimes in Lake Placid, but mostly I would be in Bulgaria with Mimi, back at Neshka Robeva's training facility, where I had trained with Lucy a few years earlier.

The local Bulgarian girls had a different training method and mentality about them. I didn't relate to them because: (1) I didn't speak their language; (2) they all had each other and shared a special bond; and (3) I didn't have the energy to try to make friends. The occasional gymnast from the U.S. or back home in Toronto would come and go, but never for long periods like me. There weren't cellphones (or at least ones that would work internationally) back then. There was one communal computer for all the athletes to use, but the internet never worked. I would buy phone cards with whatever money I could scrounge to attempt to call my mom. The pay phone in the Bulgarian training facility was terrible and I could never get through, so eventually I just gave up. Besides, hearing my mother's voice made me even sadder.

I missed everything about back home and was tired of living out of a suitcase and washing my clothes in the sink. I was borderline depressed and entered a dark place. All I wanted was to sleep. It became harder and harder to get out of bed in the morning for first practice or after my afternoon nap before second practice. I was weak, and every day my purpose seemed further and further away. I felt as though the Olympics would never come. I would count down every minute like a countdown to New Year's Eve just to feel one step closer to achieving my dreams and being done. Done with the pressure, strain, and my Olympic dream, and finally able to be normal and sleep as long as I wanted and eat whatever I wanted. I went days without speaking. I would simply wake up alone, train alone, eat (whatever minimal food I was allowed) alone, and sleep alone. It was isolating. It was as though I'd turned a switch in my brain to autopilot so I could get through the final months leading up to the Games. It didn't help that Mimi acted different toward me in her hometown. I guess it was like a high school reunion for her and she had to "show off" to her peers. I felt like an embarrassment to her half the time, but I know she was just trying to mould me into the best possible gymnast I could be. She had the best intentions, but I found training in a foreign country difficult.

The regimen was also extremely strict. Let's talk diet and weight in the gymnastic world again. Gymnasts were weighed at least twice a day, typically after meals to see if you ate too much or were sneaking food at night. I often skipped drinking water in order to weigh under for the day. Maintaining a low weight, or losing weight, essentially being as skinny as possible, was the goal. Often, if you were heavier at a competition, you would drop in ranking, almost like a punishment, even if you performed with no mistakes. My weight would fluctuate because the food was different. I would hide food in my pillowcase or under my mattress because there was nowhere to go if you were starving late at night and had to skip dinner because you weighed over that day.

Despite the intensity of this period of my life, I have little or no recollection of the details. My teammates from that time often reminisce about our times in Bulgaria or international competitions, but I don't have any recollection whatsoever of those events. It's probably some form of post-traumatic stress disorder, and the fact that I shut down to cope and get through each day leading up to the Games contributed to my memory loss. I think it is a strength of mine. But some might argue that it's not a healthy way to go about coping.

In March of 2004, I competed at the Olympic Test Event in Greece. I placed eighth all around and ninth in finals. Later that year I placed tenth at the Thiais Grand Prix, silver at the Shishmanova World Cup, and eleventh at the Varna World Cup in Bulgaria. I was consistent and continued to hold my place internationally. I also won five gold medals at the Pacific Alliance Championships in Honolulu (this time for the U.S.).

After the Pacific Alliance, other athletes and I were flown to Los Angeles to do a photoshoot for the *Vanity Fair* Olympics issue. However, the day before getting on the plane, I took a day to relax on the beach and got a severe sunburn on every part of my body. I was a tomato when I arrived on set. Thank God the photos were in black and white. It is an iconic image to me, and one that I look back on often. This photoshoot was one of my first experiences of feeling glamorous and like a star. I loved being in front of the camera. It was like day and night to my reality as a gymnast. I knew I wanted more of this in my life.

And because life is often complicated, the year before at the World Championship, I had qualified the U.S. for a spot to compete in Athens, but not myself personally. I still had to compete at the Olympic Trials in San Jose in June of 2004. Two months before the Olympics, I had to re-earn my place. There's a reason that the organizers do this. Let's say a year prior I had qualified myself for a spot in the Olympics. Then a year later I've gained one hundred pounds and barely trained, but because I qualified a year ago, I am able to compete at the Olympic Games. So, they have the athlete qualify their country for a spot, but not the individual, because the federations want to ensure that when you compete at the Olympics you are at your peak physical ability and still number one in your country.

I understood this approach, but it just felt like another roadblock I had to push through. In the end it was a beautiful competition, and NBC did a wonderful special on my father and me that I still watch. I took the gold at the Olympic Trials, but there was some fierce competition from fellow American gymnasts Olga Karmansky and Lisa Wang, who were right behind me and kept me on my toes.

I flew home briefly following the Olympic Trials to repack before returning to Bulgaria one last time before the Olympics. It was a very nerve-racking and exciting time. I was two months away from my dream. My whole life had been leading up to this point. Graciously, Annely threw an Olympics going-away party for me at her house. It was a lovely gesture, but in reality, almost no one showed up from my club. I was grateful for the few gymnasts and parents who did attend to show me their support, but it was hard not seeing the girls I'd spent years training and competing with see me off in my final days, the very same girls who once came over for sleepovers and dressed up and sang along to Spice Girls with me. Regardless, Annely always had a way of bringing love and light into any situation, and she sent me off with grace and support.

While I was home, I was also informed that for the first time ever, I was going to have my very own cheering section to watch me compete in Athens that consisted of my mother and brothers, my uncle John, and my aunt Peggy. My friend Laura, who I met at church, and who was going to be my roommate at university, also came, as did John, my brother's best friend, who took me to my prom.

After this whirlwind visit, I returned to Bulgaria for the final month and a half of training. I was not allowed to stay in the village prior to competing, because Mimi feared it would be a distraction. I was not happy with this decision, because the Olympic village is a big part of the experience. But in my sport, our coaches kept us under lock and key with little interaction with the outside world to distract us. It was, of course, extremely lonely and depressing as I mentioned, and I couldn't wait to arrive in the village. Granted, I was competing on the final day of competition, so in hindsight maybe she was right to keep me in Bulgaria, even though I felt like I was slowly dying inside.

It was back to the gruelling *Groundhog Day* routine of sleep, eat, train, ballet, sleep, eat, train, ballet. By this time I had found an internet café in the town that was full of heavy smokers. I didn't care because at least I could communicate with friends and family back home. It helped ease the solitude. I would eat salted almonds there, which didn't help maintain my weight. My coach did her best to get me ready for the Games, but we struggled to find the balance. I think by this point we were both exhausted.

I flew to Athens for the opening ceremonies, which gave me the last push and motivation that I needed. They gave me multiple duffel bags of USA Roots swag gear. It was incredible. When we all marched out in our uniforms, the crowd roaring and the fireworks going off just made my insides tingle in ways I'd never felt before. It was that Olympics feeling. It's a feeling that is indescribable. You're surrounded by excellence everywhere you look, and you know you all share a very special bond. The only downfall was that my shoes were a little too small and I returned to Bulgaria with lots of blisters on my heels. which my coach wasn't too pleased about, but I didn't care because that one night was worth the pain.

I had over two weeks left to train in Bulgaria before I flew back to Athens. These were very long weeks. My coach was pushing me, I was doing my best, but I felt as though my body was just not listening. I was tired, burnt out, and mentally beaten down. I wasn't in my top physical shape either. Maybe it was one too many salty almonds at the internet café, but whatever had caused my weight gain, I remember sticking toothpicks under the scale to weigh under. It was a trick that the Bulgarian girls taught me. When the scale is off-kilter, it can make the dial on the scale lower. I was desperate and wanting to get to Athens at all costs.

By this point my coach and I were ready for the journey to be over. We weren't talking much as we had spent so much time together training long hours every day. We got to Athens, and it all happened so quickly. I had a few practices that went well. I wandered the village in my free time. I enjoyed meeting the athletes and laughing with them. I felt like they brought me back to life. I especially remember meeting Jennie Finch in the physio room. Jennie was also featured in the *Vanity Fair* article with me, and I felt so honoured to be in the same room as her. She was just drop-dead gorgeous and a rockstar of a softball player. She filled a room with so much energy it was incredible, and I felt myself feeding off her positive vibes.

As with all international rhythmic gymnastics competitions, day one is the qualification round using two of the apparatuses, usually ball and hoop. Day two of the qualification round is the remaining two apparatuses, ribbon and clubs. From there you get ranked. The goal is to place high enough to make it to finals, and only two per country are allowed in the finals. I was the sole American because our country only qualified one spot. Some countries like Russia, Bulgaria, or Ukraine had three gymnasts competing, and of course, Greece was granted multiple athletes (who I always ranked ahead of prior to the Games) as the host country. And now we are back to where this chapter began ... Day one of my Olympics debut.

O

I do my best, but I'm a little shaky during my ball routine. Nothing obvious, and no major mistakes, but I know it isn't the best ball routine I've ever done. My scores aren't great, but they aren't bad either. I wave to my family and friends in the crowd as they cheer me on. One down and three more routines to go. All in all, I feel I got the jitters out, and I go backstage to warm up for my hoop routine. Hoop is my best event as I have the highest difficulty, and it is my dance routine. I love it and am excited to showcase it on this level. As I warm up, I take a minute and say all the Bible verses my mother gave me. I need this routine to go well.

As I make my way to the competition floor, drying my palms with a towel, I take a few deep breaths, and I am ready. I step out onto the floor, scared because this is my most risky and difficult routine, but I know I'm prepared, and it's my chance. I continue through the routine with ease, and I catch my hardest skill by the skin of my teeth. It is a skill where I throw the hoop, do two vertical rotations, fall to my knees, and do a walkover and catch the hoop completely blind in a bridge with one leg up. But I'm a millimetre from kicking that hoop across the entire floor — it's a very close call. It is at that moment I know *I got this*. I continue throughout the routine dancing, smiling, and catching everything. I nail it. The crowd goes wild, and I wave again to my family and friends.

I sit down in the kiss-and-cry area, where athletes blow kisses to the camera and the audience and cry out of happiness or sadness depending on their performance and scores. You can't escape the kiss-and-cry; they make you sit there and react to your scores.

I sit there with a camera in my face, Mimi hugs me. The scores take longer than normal to appear, which I think is strange. Typically, when scores take a while, it means the judges are meeting because there is too big a discrepancy. The scores finally appear and are two points lower than what I typically receive for this event. My facial expression immediately goes from very happy with my routine to completely distraught. I want to get up and leave, but the organizers tell me I can't because I'm on live television. It's terrible, I'm furious, I want to scream. How could I have been judged so unfairly? I soon realize that this isn't going to be a fair competition. There are Greek girls ahead of me at this point, and I had placed in front of them at every international competition where I had ever competed. I get that we are in their hometown and Athens is the host of the Games, but the politics are very evident.

I pack up my things, completely angry, and head back to the village. I call my mom from the village and just cry. For once my emotions are free-flowing. I tell her I don't want to compete the next day and I'm done. Technically, I am already an Olympian. What's the point of competing in my other two events when my scores are so low for routines that I hit? My mother calms me down by telling me, "You are not competing for scores; you are competing for God and for your father looking down on you. You are here to show the world how far you've come and to do it for yourself and no one else." I hate that she is so right because I'm so mad.

Thanks to my mother and her advice the night before, I get up the next day, August 26, 2004, on my nineteenth birthday, do my hair and makeup, and proceed to the facility for day two to compete with clubs and ribbon. I warm up and tape up my toe because the first round is ribbon. It's my worst event; it requires a lot of pirouettes, which is tough on my turf toe. I spray so much freeze spray on my toe that I can't feel half of my right foot. This is how I get through my ribbon routine. I proceed to the competition area, present to the judges, and perform my ribbon routine out of spite. My first skill is the hardest; once I get through that I have more confidence. I continue to do my best and leap, turn, and do my tricks through the pain, and it goes extremely well. I'm relieved, I've hit three of three routines by now. I have one more to go. My score is essentially the same as my hoop score, which proves how corrupt the judging is. I always score at least one point lower with ribbon than hoop, which isn't the case at this competition. I laugh it off and head backstage. I am not competing for scores or rankings anymore, I am competing for myself.

Next, I warm up for my final routine. Clubs. I like this routine a lot. It is a fast, dynamic, and serious routine, and I always score high with it. My difficulty is up there with my hoop routine, and I feel it's a good routine to end on. This time I enter the floor with more confidence than ever before. I am determined to hit all four of my routines and make it as difficult as possible for these judges to screw me over.

The music starts and I am off on a mission. Nailing skill after skill, moving faster and stronger than ever before. I have fire in my eyes. I don't feel any pain in my toe. I feel like I'm on a high. I am almost done with my dream. I am almost done with the blood, sweat, and tears. I am almost a true Olympian. I gear up for my final throw to end my routine. Every purpose in my life is counting on this moment. I throw one club in the air and do a vertical 360-degree turn and walkover to my knees, a move that makes me lose sight of the club, while I hold the other club in my hand. I pray that the one in the air is going to land perfectly as I trap the club on the floor with the one in my hand and perform a chest cartwheel on the ground simultaneously. Then I throw my other club and do a breakdance-like move, catch it, and smile from ear to ear, and shoot that fire in my eyes right at the judges in my final pose. I am never one to celebrate publicly or show emotion after a routine, but I fist-pump so hard in this moment. I did it! I nailed four of four routines on the Olympic stage. I present quickly to the judges as I am so done with their opinions. I wave to the audience and my family and friends as their encouragement is what got me through this competition. I blow a kiss to my dad and point to him in heaven right on the competition mat before I exit to the kiss-and-cry area. Mimi and I embrace each other. All tensions that once were, are gone. We did it, we made it to the Olympics. My scores appear and they are higher (not by much) than my other three events. I say "finally" to the camera laughing, implying that it takes four tries to get a fair score. I hug my coach one last time and exit the kiss-and-cry area for good.

O

You probably want to know where I ended up on the scoreboard. Well, I finished fifteenth overall. I was twelfth in clubs, fourteenth in ball, sixteenth in ribbon, and nineteenth in hoop. Not my best finish, but that wasn't due to my performance. It was beyond my control, and I accepted that. The trouble with judged sports is that you are subject to their opinions, and it can be political depending on what flag you represent. Over the years I had my fair share of politics to deal with, it just came with the sport. Regardless, I was proud of myself. My father would be proud, my mother and family were proud. My coach and the USA Gymnastics Federation were proud of me. That was all that mattered.

Afterward my family and I celebrated at the Bank of America House, where they would provide free meals to the family members of the U.S. Olympians. It was amazing. I ate more than I ever had

MARY SANDERS

before. My family kept watching me eat like I hadn't eaten in years. After that I prepared for the closing ceremonies.

The closing ceremonies were one of the best experiences of my athletic career. I remember crying tears of joy throughout it all. I walked with new friends I had made in the village, traded pins with athletes from other countries, took lots of selfies on my disposable camera, and celebrated a dream come true. I was an Olympian, and no one could ever take that away from me — no one. It was a beautiful conclusion to my third life.

## What I Learned

**Reason:** My reason to get out of bed and thrive was to push myself to the limit to make it across the finish line to Olympic glory.

**Reinvent:** In this third life, the reinvention was more subtle. I was still a rhythmic gymnast, but I had literally grown up. I'm sure that going from thirteen to nineteen, as I did in this span of time, entailed plenty of reinvention. I solidified more of who I was, grew more confident, and took ownership of my life.

**Right:** You must learn not to care so much what others think. It is your right to make decisions for you, in your own interest. That was what I learned during this phase of my life when I had to choose between remaining on the Canadian team, where I was unlikely to achieve my goal, or switching to the American team, where I had a chance. My decision made me unpopular, but it was my right to exercise it. And I have no regrets. I feel we regret more the chances we don't take, than those we do.

O

Life Three, an Olympian, was complete. Next up, Life Four ...

70

# 4TH LIFE:

## ACROBAT

---

I stand on the edge of a bed in total darkness. But I'm not alone. Another performer perches nearby. Across the stage two other performers wait on a second bed. We are dressed in pajamas, mine are pink. My long hair is in two braids. We have practised for six months for this moment to debut our "bouncing bed" act in front of a live audience. There are other performers on stage with roles to play who will exit the stage, leaving we four acrobats as the focus. I take a deep breath. My nerves tingle with excitement. The lights come on and the music starts. I have a split second to take in the hushed crowd. Then there is no time for anything except to hit my mark. We pretend to be kids jumping and leaping from bed to bed, throwing pillows at each other, and performing high-flying tricks in between as the audience gasps, cheers, and claps. The climax of the act nears, and I perform "spotters," which is ten to twelve back handsprings in a row in one spot on the tiny bed, without hitting my feet or head on the railings on either end. The crowd loves it. It is my specialty move. It is April 2005. A circus tent in Montreal feels a lifetime away from the Olympic stage in Athens. Yet here I am.

O

After the Olympics I returned home to Mississauga with the expectation that I'd begin university in January 2005. But first I had to hit the road. Before Athens I had accepted an invitation to join an American production called the Tour of Gymnastics Champions in September. The prospect of the tour was what propelled me through my last few weeks of solitary training in Bulgaria. These tours are very lucrative, and for the first time in my life it meant an income and saving money. Plus, I was so excited to perform, yet not compete!

But first there was adjusting to life after Athens. I wasn't expecting a parade or glamorous party. After all, my send-off hadn't exactly been a sellout affair. Here's what no one tells you or prepares you for: When an athlete has achieved their goal of an Olympic appearance, and if they don't medal, and are retiring from sport, there's a sadness that sweeps over. At least, that was my experience. I was drained. Physically, mentally, and emotionally. With the tour fast approaching, I didn't have a lot of time to come to terms with any of it. And I had one important event to attend before leaving town: My mother's wedding to Rick.

The event was held in the party room of the townhouse complex where Rick and my mother lived, and where I stayed when I was in town. The reception was not extravagant, but it was a nice evening of food, dinner, and dancing. We all had a few too many that night (and I was a major lightweight just coming off of the Olympics) and a few of us hopped the fence and ended up in the complex pool, which was a lot of fun. That is, until the cops showed up and ordered us to get out or get arrested. It was well worth it; it was the send-off I needed before departing the next day. When I said my goodbyes, I didn't think my mother was unhappy, and of course she always played it cool like everything was fine. And to her, in that moment, it was.

In hindsight, I should have been there more for her throughout the weeks leading up to her big day to help plan the event, maybe I could have changed what happened. Though that's doubtful. I mean, I was a nineteen-year-old athlete, one who was unable to cope with her own post-Olympics mental health, what did I know about love and marriage? However, there were plenty of red flags about Rick along the way that everyone in my family chose to ignore. And as was the case since I was a child, no one was sharing their feelings. Like my brothers and I didn't tell our mom that we hated Stan, we also didn't let our true feelings and doubts about Rick be known either. Our family pattern of bottling up emotions continued, and with disturbing consequences for my mother.

As for those doubts and red flags, for starters, Rick had an excuse for everything. He told my mother, and us, that he made good money at his sales job. He didn't. That was why my aunt and uncle paid for my mom to travel to Athens. Her multiple jobs went into supporting herself and Rick. That was just one example. To put it bluntly, he was a narcissistic pathological liar. He also attended church like a saint, sometimes multiple times a week if you include Bible study. The women at church knew him and said he was a good man. His "good Christian" act played a major role in getting my mother to trust him. After all, how could a man of God ever betray her? Not even God could save my mother from the irreversible damage and trauma Rick caused in their marriage. But I'm getting ahead of myself.

O

The Tour of Gymnastics Champions was scheduled to run until November 28, but it ended up getting extended into December due to sold-out shows. It was a forty-state tour across America showcasing the men and women artistic gymnasts as well as trampoline, acrobatic, and rhythmic Olympians from Athens. Picture "stars on ice" but for gymnastics. Carly Patterson had taken home the all-around individual gold in artistic gymnastics and the women's team had finished second overall. Carly was a superstar; she spearheaded our tour, and everyone wanted to see her in action.

A typical twenty-four hours unfolded like this: We did a show, got on the bus and drove to wherever the next performance would be, checked into a hotel in the middle of the night, slept all morning, headed to the arena, and performed like rockstars. After the show we hopped back on the bus and did it all over again. Day in, day out. Most nights, we partied on the bus after the show. There were lots of buses. If memory serves, there were about three for the performers. A girl bus, which was the anti-party bus because some of the girls were minors and had a chaperone, a boy bus, and then the circus and dancer bus. You can imagine which was the most fun! There were another five or so buses for the crew, who rotated throughout the tour, spending time on each bus to get to know everyone. The clash between coming off the strict Olympic regime and this freeing reality was intoxicating to me, as was the high we got performing every night to sold-out arenas. I wasn't even the star of the show, Carly was, but I still felt like one, we all did.

Besides the gymnasts the performance included backup dancers and two circus artists, an aerial silk performer, and an aerial hoop performer. Watching these two aerialists was my first true glimpse into circus work. Watching them fly through the air had me as mesmerized as the audience. I didn't realize in those first few months how much of an impact the circus artists would have on my life, but I knew one day I wanted to choreograph and direct one of these shows.

My own segments were a blast for me and, I hope, the audience. Performing was always my favourite part of competing, so being able to dance and perform "showy" elements (like the illusion I described earlier) rather than difficult high-scoring skills was my dream. The tour gave me an opportunity to show off every night with dim lights, lots of flashes of cameras, and a crowd going crazy over the smallest moves. I did a solo routine to a Coldplay song called "Clocks." I still get chills every time I hear the song. I loved it. I loved performing and I realized on tour that this was my passion.

I gained about twenty-five pounds during those three months and I didn't care. Granted, I was underweight going in from strict dieting, so to the average person I probably looked like a normal, healthy nineteen-year-old. Also, the men on the tour liked the new plus-twenty-five-pound Mary better and I started to like the attention. I dated one of the dancers and felt like a real superstar.

The upside to such freedom was finally giving my body permission to fully develop after all the years of doing everything I could to stop puberty. I initially got my period at fifteen when I had put on a few pounds. Then when I lost all the weight, my period stopped. But puberty hit me hard and fast on the tour. My hormones were all over the place, and I wasn't sure what was going on. It was like I was nineteen going on thirteen.

There was limited supervision, too. Gone were my strict coaches, replaced by buffets and room service. We were free — a group of gymnasts mostly under twenty living life on the road like a rock band. We partied, laughed, and became an instant family. It was like a dream, and I never wanted to do anything else. I wanted to live on that tour bus forever.

On one of our rare nights off, a group of us got tattoos of the Olympic rings. It felt very rebellious to me, because tattoos weren't exactly big in my family, and it remains my only one. I had the artist ink my lower right hip so that I could hide it if need be. Other gymnasts got it on their wrists, backs, ankles, and necks, to show it off. It hurt but the pain was worth it, a permanent reminder and symbol of the hard work. In a way it marked my first twenty years of life, the sacrifices and the joys.

Of course, we didn't really think it through, because we had to keep performing while making sure the tattoos didn't get infected. It was tough doing shows with open wounds in areas of the body that are vital to specific gymnastics moves. But that was only one complication. We also discovered that a tattoo of the rings was frowned upon by the Olympic Committee because it is a trademarked logo. We dismissed the issue because countless other Olympians rocked the rings. We were Olympians, first and foremost, and would remain so forever. To this day, if someone refers to me as a "former Olympian," I correct them by saying, "once an Olympian, always an Olympian." It's the simple truth.

O

During the tour a Cirque du Soleil scout named Dana Brass came to watch one of our shows. Unbeknownst to me, Cirque had also sent a scout to watch me compete in Athens. When the Tour of Champions came to Vegas, Dana took me to see *O*. I was stunned and flattered. I sat in the best seats, and Dana took me backstage where I met some of the lighting designers and watched parts of the show from the automation desk, which was impressive to say the least. The whole night was a VIP experience to get me excited about joining the circus troupe. It worked. After the show ended, I turned to Dana and said, "Where do I sign up?"

The actual decision was more complicated. University had always been the plan. But I never wanted to go back to the financial struggles we had growing up. I wanted to look forward and be successful, not only in my career, but also in being able to provide for my family one day. Indeed, while the Tour of Champions didn't pay a lot of money, it was enough to help my family out a little and buy my first house, an investment property in Mississauga. I put the minimum deposit down on a townhouse in the same complex where my mother lived and rented it out. I had no plans to live there, since I was going to be in London, Ontario, at school, or so I thought.

Now, as I stood in Vegas, backstage at Cirque, it was clear to me that there was this whole prosperous world of entertainment waiting for me. Cirque meant performing (which I loved) and a steady income (which I craved), and it made me rethink the university plan. Why take on enormous student debt, as my brothers had for their degrees, when I really didn't even know what I wanted to be when I grew up? Especially when I could start making money now. Not exactly the path most people would take, but everyone's journey is different. If you follow your heart and your passions, I believe that will always lead to success. And success comes in many forms, but for me in that moment, success meant money. Lots of it, or more than I would ever attain if I went to university for the next four years. And just like that, without really knowing what I signed up for, I ran away and joined the circus to begin my fourth life: Acrobat.

This felt like a full-circle moment for me. My love of Cirque came from watching a performance of *Alegria* when I was a child. The contortionists inspired me to stretch and become more flexible, which became part of my gymnastic routine once I switched to rhythmic. In the *Vanity Fair* article, the journalist had written, "When it's time for her to retire from competition she hopes to take her skills to the top — the big top, that is — by joining the arty troupe of Cirque du Soleil."

When the Tour of Champions ended, I returned home to my mother's townhouse to unpack and repack, this time for a move to Montreal where I would live at the Cirque du Soleil headquarters and join the circus troupe for their new 2005 creation, *Corteo*. It was a two-and-a-half-year contract to perform in a group trampoline act. I thought it was fitting because my father was a trampolinist.

The concept of *Corteo* was the death of a clown, envisioning his funeral, and what it would look like on his way to the afterlife. Cirque is often abstract, but *Corteo* was directed by Daniele Finzi Pasca, an Italian who was very driven by the realness and emotion of the performance. *Corteo*, although it was realistic, was also was magical. There were giants, little people, talking golf balls, angels, and a real-life clown who was dead and dreaming of his funeral, which we were all part of. We were not clowns hiding under white makeup, we were recognizable on stage, and for the first time ever in Cirque du Soleil's history, *Corteo* revealed the people under the makeup and costumes. I believe that is what made the first cast of *Corteo* so special. We were real people, creating a show based on who we were. Even as members of the cast came and went, the original artist was who the casting directors based their recruitment on. In a way, I feel that my heart lives on in that show.

I arrived in Montreal on December 5, 2004, with multiple suitcases, not knowing when I would return home again. The dorms were across the street from the headquarters where all the magic happened. Our rooms had walls that were paper thin, and you could literally hear everything going on with your neighbours. I could hear the giggles and yelling of artists who'd clearly been living there for months already. Everyone seemed very happy, comfortable, and at ease with one another and here I was, a fish out of water again, just like I had felt when I switched to rhythmic gymnastics or started a new school. The rooms were tiny. The bed was in the kitchen. There was a television, but it had maybe one or two channels, no cable. The bathroom had only a shower, and it was the kind that would splash everywhere, even in the toilet, because there was no shower curtain or glass window to separate the two. It wasn't exactly the height of glamour, but I had lived in worse conditions when competing in Europe. It was nice to have a stable home for the next six months, something I never had in my childhood with all the commotion at home or constant travelling.

On my first day, I walked into the studio and my eyes immediately landed on a man who felt familiar, yet I had never met him. His name was Dominic; he was older than me, and he wore glasses with thick dark frames. There was something mysterious about him, and as the days turned into weeks, we often just stared at each other, and if we passed in the halls, we locked eyes and smiled without ever talking. It was a few weeks into my time there that I learned he was the technical director on *Corteo*. Then naturally, he started to talk to me professionally about the trampoline, how it felt, what they could do to improve it, etc. But the flirting in the halls or after rehearsals while I was eating in the cafeteria continued. I knew he had a girlfriend, since I often saw them together in the halls, because she also worked at Cirque. You could say I developed a crush, and I always looked forward to seeing him. I was nineteen and he was thirty-two.

Back to that first day. I was welcomed by Cirque representatives and taken on a tour. It was a huge building with various training facilities, offices, cafeterias, physiotherapy rooms, costume shops, mailrooms, makeup rooms, and prop sets. It was mind-blowing how they did everything in-house. They had professionals from all over the world who specialized in many different areas, so they were able to do all of the necessary set design, research, and training in their local headquarters. It was a well-oiled machine; they knew exactly what they were doing and were knocking out show after show.

I proceeded to do my artist intake physical, which is mandatory for all new artists to document what physical shape they arrived in. This type of exam continues throughout an artist's time with Cirque to note the progress or injuries that occur during their tenure with the company. I wasn't in great shape because I had done minimal exercise during the Champions Tour other than my three-minute solo number and had gained quite a bit of weight. I struggled with my cardio and strength test. Initially, the physiotherapists were worried because my physicality was not what they thought it should be, but I quickly adapted and started to get in better shape as the weeks progressed. I watched as the other acrobats worked out before practice and eventually started to adopt their routine and eat healthier. In hindsight, I was a bit lazy at this point in my life. I had come off an entire life of constant training and discipline, I just wanted to have fun.

It was on my second day that I met my teammates who would be in the trampoline act, dubbed "the bouncing beds," with me. There were four of us. As I described earlier, the concept was kids jumping and playing between two beds instead of going to sleep, with lots of tricks going on between them. My partners in the act were from all over the world. There was Gustavo from Brazil, Edesia or "Edi" from Spain, and Mitch, a fellow Canadian. Gustavo and I were the youngest by about twelve years. Mitch and Edi were a couple and came to *Corteo* after they left another Cirque show. That's typically what artists did after they completed a long stint on one show, they jumped over to a different one to keep things fresh and interesting. We were quite the random combination, but Cirque knew what they were doing. It was almost like all four of us needed to have such different backgrounds to bring a unique approach to the act. Mitch was a trampolinist and comedic clown, Gustavo was a high-flying, hot-blooded daredevil, and Edi was also a rhythmic gymnast but had character training like Mitch, so she helped me a lot with the acting side of things. Then there was me, just a rhythmic gymnast straight from the Olympic Games who hadn't been on a trampoline in ten years. We became very close and created an original trampoline bed act that is still travelling the world and being performed in *Corteo* today.

But it wasn't an easy journey. On top of creating our act from scratch on an apparatus none of us had any experience with, I had to attend clown workshops, get aerial harness training, learn songs and rhythms, support other acts as an extra, and go to physiotherapy and conditioning sessions. Then it was made clear that my job went beyond my one act, I was to be part of a "house troupe," meaning I wasn't a specialty artist doing one act in the show, I had to do many things to contribute to the entire show. It was a big change for me. I was used to being a soloist on the competition floor, so joining a group act and being a "house troupe" member didn't really sit well with me. It was intense, and part of me wondered what I had gotten myself into.

One aspect of Cirque du Soleil that everyone can agree on is that the costume and makeup designs are stunning. The makeup artists designed your character and taught you how to do your makeup. I loved every part of this process. They provided a step-by-step routine that you took on the road with you. It was a two-hour makeup job each time. It was long, and if you tried to cut any corners, it was telling, and you got dinged for it, sort of like three strikes you're out, and you lost pay for one show or something. I never saw that happen, but it was incentive enough to follow step by step. Even the men had to learn how to apply makeup, and it was very funny, because often they didn't remove it properly and were walking around with eyeliner in the real world without knowing why they were getting extra attention. All of our skin took a real beating those first few months because we weren't used to wearing such thick makeup. Needless to say, I needed to up my skincare routine.

My training days were packed. It was five days a week (sometimes six days as we got closer to the premiere) with a strict, regimented schedule, and it was exhausting. My body was still trying to recover from a lifetime of training and multiple injuries, back pain, turf toe, arthritis throughout the majority of my joints, neck pain, ankle pain — essentially, despite being nineteen, my body more closely resembled someone in their forties or fifties. And the trampoline apparatus was unforgiving. It felt more like a barbed wire spring with a piece of foam on top and railings at either end, like headboards for a bed. It was about six feet wide and six feet long. This was a new design, and we were the guinea pigs. There were times I couldn't train at all because I had either sprained my ankle or thrown my back out. My core wasn't strong enough to support the intense jumping. In time, the props team added more padding, but we all had to endure some serious injuries before that happened. That's what creation of these shows is all about, trial and error. This trampoline act most definitely had its fair share of error.

In between training sessions and during our off hours, we had fun at our dorms and in the common areas. We were a family, all training and living under the same roof with minimal supervision. A little bit like the Tour of Champions except with less structure. We threw parties, had sleepovers, watched movies, and played games. We went on road trips to the grocery store and downtown Montreal to shop, eat, or go to the movies. We made the best of whatever time off we had. Sometimes it was too much fun and we had to contend with brutal hangovers to start our week.

This may sound strange, but one of the biggest surprises, I'll even go so far as to say culture shocks, was that from this point forward, I had to prepare all my own meals. There was a cafeteria where I could purchase food, but that got pricey, and I was only receiving a few hundred dollars per week during the creation period. Eventually, I learned to take the shuttle to the grocery store once a week and buy food with everyone else. There wasn't Uber or anything like ridesharing back in those days and no one could afford a car or taxi, so we piled onto shuttles that were provided by Cirque.

Grocery shopping at nineteen was something I had *never* done before, and it was extremely foreign to me. I never went grocery shopping with my mom because I hated the temptation of all the yummy foods around me that I could never eat. All my meals as a gymnast were prepared and dictated for me. All my meals on tour were provided or ordered through room service. I had no idea what I was doing and definitely struggled to drop the weight while becoming more domesticated all at the same time. I'm not sure what was more of a circus, me in my dorm kitchen or me in the actual Cirque du Soleil show.

Alcohol and drug use really wasn't spoken of, but there was definitely a work hard/play hard mentality from the get-go, with many of the coaching staff taking part. No one got a slap on the wrist unless they showed up late or missed practice. It was an environment where nothing was forbidden as long as you showed up and got your job done. We were expected to think outside the box, perform outside the box, and be pure entertainment. For some of us who were shy, this didn't come easy. I can see how substance abuse would help a person get over stage fright. Remember, most acrobats came from sport, not acting or circus school, so we were often forced outside our comfort zone to put on the best show and make the audience feel something. Nobody will pay big money to watch a robot-like person do flips. Performers need to have facial expressions and a wow factor.

Of course, I'm sure if Cirque's head office or the coaches had known about the parties, or if there had been an incident, they would have said something, but we were adults and allowed to live our lives how we saw fit. I never got into drugs at Cirque. Even though my drug testing days were over, it was far from my mind, and I never felt the urge to try anything. I think Edi, the other rhythmic performer in my act, had a lot to do with that. She was almost like a mother figure to me in the beginning, watching over me. Given that she had worked with Cirque for more than ten years, she knew the temptations that lay ahead. She had seen it all. And while she and Mitch threw a lot of the parties, I didn't always go, or if I did, I left early. I was focused, so I didn't feel any temptation to experiment with drugs. I did drink alcohol, most of us did, but even in that I was a lightweight. Then again, most of the North Americans had a hard time keeping up with the Russian and eastern European acrobats and their love of vodka. They could down shots like it was juice and be completely fine the next day at practice. Vodka was their cure for everything, even the common cold and flu. They concocted a potion made of vodka laced with an exorbitant amount of pepper that was supposed to kill the germs. I tried it once, but it didn't help, though it made me forget about my cold for a little while.

Like the gymnastic tour, Cirque was a bubble. And because of the tour, I had arrived three months later than everyone else, so by the time I showed up, everyone had either coupled up or had their partners with them. There were some performers who had multiple relationships, which caused drama within the group. Like any environment where people reside under the same roof for long periods of time, there's always going to be attraction and temptation. Any sort of cheating or straying always came to light; it is nearly impossible for anyone to keep a secret when you are surrounded by the same people day in and day out.

All this is to say that, as usual, I struggled to find where I belonged. I was only nineteen, so I found it challenging at times to relate to many of the performers who were older and more experienced than I was. And of course, these familiar feelings of isolation brought all the insecurities that stemmed from school and not having a core group of friends flooding back. Luckily, we were so busy creating and training that there wasn't too much time to dwell. And we were about to leave on our North American tour, even if the show still had some hiccups to work through. I was excited about the prospect of being on the road again, given that I'd loved the Tour of Champions experience so much. However, the next two years unfolded in very different ways, and the naive girl who arrived in Montreal was forever altered.

As we neared the premiere date for *Corteo,* it became clear that we weren't ready. We had spent 80 percent of the six-month creation period preparing for the first act and not giving the second act much love. Act one was forty-five minutes with a thirty-minute intermission, followed by act two, which was another forty-five minutes. My trampoline act was in act one and was second in the lineup. But as a house troupe member, I had to participate in other aspects of the show, singing, dancing, dressing up as a horse (yes, really), setting up and tearing down equipment. Not exactly as glamorous a job as it was made out to be. I got more tired doing the house troupe tasks than my actual act. I envied the soloists that went on stage for five minutes and wowed the audience and then kicked back and relaxed until it was time for the final bows. That was what I wanted.

Premieres for big-top touring shows typically premiered in Montreal. Local audiences were more forgiving about seeing a show in its early stages. Their reviews could be harsh but always constructive, so the directors knew what changes to make before they embarked on international territory. We did a few soft openings where family, friends, and other staff were invited to watch, and these went quite well, and we had positive feedback. It felt amazing to finally be on stage and performing in front of live audiences. I loved that they could recognize our faces because we weren't hiding under white clown makeup. I was still Mary, but with dramatic stage makeup.

And finally, we started to be paid per show, which was much more lucrative than receiving the training stipend. We made minor changes leading up to the big premiere, and we all felt ready. So ready. I would say the intensity of a premiere is a lot like leading up to a big competition. This time, though, I was part of a team, and it wasn't just me, myself, and I preparing. It was nice to feel the vibe and energy of everyone around me.

Premiere day arrived on April 21, 2005, and we had a few last-minute rehearsals before Guy Laliberté, the CEO and founder of Cirque du Soleil, arrived to give us a pep talk. He had founded Cirque in 1984 and had been a street performer himself. Guy left Cirque as CEO in April 2015, but still maintains a stake in the business and continues to provide strategic and creative input to the company. He still makes headlines for his many interests. He's an avid traveller, investor, and poker player, and in 2009 he became the first Canadian space tourist. He dedicated his trip to space to raising awareness about the water issues facing humanity. While his trip to space was controversial, it literally proved that the sky was not the limit for him.

To pump us up for the premiere, Guy gave us one of the most motivating speeches I've ever heard (I could have used a speech like this prior to competing at the Olympics), the room started to rumble, our hearts started to jump out of our chests, and we all joined hands for one last hurrah. It was time to show the world what we had been working on. We were a family, and we were about to reveal our world for the first time to the paying public.

As the curtains opened, the crowd erupted, and the journey began. Act by act, we were hitting our marks. Our trampoline bed act went off without a hitch. Throughout the show, the crowd was laughing, crying, applauding, and in complete awe at the level of skill they were witnessing. It was looking to be a perfect premiere until the unimaginable happened — a major technical glitch occurred and forced the show to stop abruptly. It seemed that a machine froze and needed to be rebooted and repaired. It wasn't a quick fix. The technicians worked fast and tirelessly, but they couldn't fix the machine in time. Guy Laliberté was yelling, everyone was frantic. But the damage was done. We didn't have a successful premiere and had to skip the act completely and move on. It just didn't feel the same. The audience was forgiving and still gave us a standing ovation, but in our hearts, we knew this wasn't a good first impression.

But I pitied the poor technicians, including Dominic, the mysterious technical director. The technicians were the real stars of the show. They worked double the number of hours we did, setting up and tearing down equipment and tents, and moving from city to city on a tour bus while we flew on commercial airplanes and got a week off in between. Yet it was expected that they would ensure a flawless show every night.

After the failed premiere, we all huddled backstage and embraced one another, disappointed, but it was beyond our control. We faced many technical difficulties throughout our tour because *Corteo* pushed the technicians to the limit. But that is what Cirque does so well, they push the boundaries of possibility. We all cried, laughed, and put it behind us. We removed our stage makeup and got ready for the premiere party. All the artists always looked forward to Cirque's extravagant parties. Red Bull was the sponsor of our premiere party this time around, and we all got so hyped up on vodka Red Bulls that none of us could sleep for days after, although we still were expected to perform to capacity.

Speaking of parties, Cirque hosted one of the craziest, most extravagant events for the 2005 Formula 1 Canadian Grand Prix at the Circuit Gilles Villeneuve during our Montreal period, before we took the show on the road to other cities. The F1 party was held at the headquarters where we trained every day, yet it was transformed into this other world for one night. I remember people on stilts, clowns, beautiful fairies, teepee tents everywhere on the lawn (which were rumored to have a different drug of choice in each), nearly naked women with sushi covering their entire bodies to eat off of, as well as nearly naked women in chocolate fountains where you could dip marshmallows or fruit. It was highly sexual but tastefully done.

We had premiere parties in every city where we performed, and they were fun, sometimes too much fun, but it was a good way to blow off steam and spend time with everyone offstage, including the technicians and other staff who we rarely spent quality time with. There was always a stigma around the artists, a perception that we were being divas while the technicians and other supporting staff were working around the clock. It's true that they worked crazy hours to support the artists and the show, and I always tried to make time to get to know them. I never wanted to be labelled a diva. After all, with my background, I was the furthest thing from it, but being on stage and receiving a lot of attention every night did make it hard not to want or even expect that level of constant attention offstage as well. We were front and centre, but the show wouldn't have been possible without everyone behind the scenes. The technicians, supporting staff, cooks, and physiotherapists were just as much a part of the show as we were. Our lives were in their hands, we trusted them, we relied on them, and we needed them to run a successful tour.

And the night of the *Corteo* premiere was when my fourth life truly began. Almost without knowing it, and certainly without consciously marking it, I had left behind the young girl gymnast who only wanted to make her father proud and honour his legacy, and welcomed the young woman who was embarking on her own life, finally able to make all the decisions — good and bad — herself.

## What I Learned

**Reason:** My reason to get out of bed and thrive was to live life on my own terms and earn money so I could be financially independent and not struggle to make ends meet.

**Reinvent:** After the Olympics my life as a gymnast was over. I had to find my next passion, and when opportunity came to me, first with the gymnastic tour, and then with Cirque du Soleil, I jumped on it. You have to take risks. That is part of reinvention, trying the hard thing, the scary new thing, and not worrying about failure.

**Right:** It was my right to not follow the standard path and go to university. Making an unconventional choice, but one that is right for you, is your right.

O

Life Four, Mary the acrobat, was born, and would grow into Life Five ...

# 5<sup>TH</sup> LIFE:

## THE SOLOIST

---

I'm on stage about to perform a skill where I link arms with another artist, then we face opposite directions and do three jumps. One of us flips front and the other flips back. I always flip front for this move. I'm nervous because on this night, my regular partner is injured and I'm about to literally take a leap of faith with a fill-in who I've never worked with. Our moment to jump comes and I glance at him, and I can tell he isn't wholly present. His eyes are glassy, he smells of alcohol, and he is twitchy and hyper. I put two and two together. But it's too late. We jump! Only he forgets which way to flip, so with arms linked we both go for the front flip and knock shoulders mid-air. Before I know it, I am upside down about to land on my head on the trampoline. In this split second, I feel a rush of terror because this is how you can break your neck. Thank God I'm so flexible; I land on my head and left shoulder with my feet over my head and roll out of it unscathed. Shaken up but not injured. My partner apologizes profusely, though he barely remembers what happened and doesn't know why he flipped the wrong way. But it is in this moment that I'm done with group acts.

○

After our premiere in Montreal, we headed out on tour. *Corteo* played in every major city across North America, doing ten shows per week with one day off, for a minimum of six weeks to three months in a single location. It was exhilarating and exhausting.

A few months into the tour, I noticed hundreds of dollars mysteriously leaving my account by cheques I hadn't written. I asked my mom to look for the chequebook that I had left in my room. Not surprisingly, she couldn't find it. At first. Eventually, it was located in the room of Rick's stepson, Christian, a name which I found quite ironic given his rather unchristian behaviour. He was forging cheques, I suspected, to deal or buy drugs at school.

Between shows we got one week off, unpaid. A lot of the acrobats went away on vacation between cities. Instead of jetting off to Paris, I returned to Mississauga to see my mother. She continued to struggle and was back working multiple jobs whenever Rick was in between salesman jobs. I wanted to find my missing money, so I traced where the cheques were being cashed in Mississauga and linked it back to my chequebook that I found in Christian's room. Rick promised to discipline him, which never happened. Not that I was entirely unsympathetic. According to Rick, he had met Christian's mother during a night out when he wasn't a churchgoing Bible-thumper. Rick legally adopted Christian at some point during this relationship, because the woman was considered an unfit mother. I never got the details, but apparently she dealt with substance abuse, and Rick told us that he helped her get clean and then he took her son in. But there were times when this woman called, especially if she needed something (money, a drive somewhere), and

Rick for some reason always obliged. Even my mother felt sorry for her. Needless to say, even with my brothers and I out of the house, my mother had her hands full with a troubled stepson. It just never got easier for my mom.

On the next week off between tour stops, I went home again, but this time there was a purpose for the visit besides just a family reunion. I had to have my wisdom teeth removed. As she always did, my mother nursed me back to health and we spent a whole week together on the sofa eating Jell-O, ice cream, and for me, Tylenol 3. It gave us a lot of quality mother-daughter time and I confessed to her about Dominic, the mysterious technical director. I had started seeing him in Montreal after he ended his previous relationship. I was excited about this blossoming romance but also needed to figure out how I could maintain a relationship when we were living two different lives. Mine was on tour, while Dominic remained in Montreal.

But it wasn't only my romantic life that I needed my mother's advice on. I wasn't happy with my job. Cirque was gruelling, yet I was also bored performing the same show every day, sometimes twice per day. I still had over a year left to go on my contract and I needed something else to motivate me and pull me through the remainder of the show dates. Cirque had an education program that paid 50 percent of your tuition, a program they set up to act like a scholarship for their acrobats to encourage them to study. While I didn't regret not going to university, I did recognize that I wanted more from my life than being an acrobat. I needed to get a degree.

My mother helped me select an online public relations program from Ryerson University (now Toronto Metropolitan University) that I could complete on tour. It was a specialized program that required a bachelor's degree prior to being accepted. I was interviewed, and based on my career and my honours average from high school, I was accepted. I supposed they treated my Olympic title as being equivalent to a bachelor's degree. I was so grateful to be starting the program. I needed something more in my life than jumping on a trampoline acting like a child.

This time when I returned to the tour, instead of attending premiere parties, I returned to my hotel room and studied. It was difficult to steer clear of the parties and to say no to the beach or shopping on days off. These outings were my social life, especially given I was so far from home and from Dominic. But it also meant I didn't spend money unnecessarily. I wanted to save every penny so I could buy my own place after the tour was over. I had my rental property, but I wanted my own condo in downtown Toronto, which was the motivation I needed to keep my head down and stay out of the darker side of tour life.

While the relationship with Dominic was getting more serious, I became disillusioned by the recklessness of some of the performers when it came to sex and relationships. There was one incident that made me realize I was not on the same "party" level as most. I was close friends with a male acrobat from Great Britain. He had a wife and kid back home; he seemed normal, down to earth, and I liked talking to him. His wife often visited, and she was the loveliest lady. We grew pretty close and stayed in touch even when she was back home.

Then one night, the entire cast was at a bar after a show. I headed to the ladies' room, where I discovered my British friend having sex at the sink with the newest acrobat to join the cast. She hadn't been there even a week, was all of ninety pounds soaking wet, and here was this guy in his mid-thirties with a family back home, hooking up with the most random and newest member of the cast. I couldn't believe what I was seeing. They were both out of their minds on some substance, but what I couldn't get out of my head was the infidelity. His thoughtlessness when his family was back home missing him didn't sit well with me. I've always had a thing about trust, which is that I don't trust many people. That could be due to daddy issues from losing my father at a young age, or watching my ex-stepfather, Stan, and current stepfather, Rick, lie and disappoint my mother.

All the tour sex had other consequences. And I had to comfort more than a few women who had to undergo abortions. Clearly, none of this was planned and they couldn't afford to take time off to have a baby, let alone after a one-night stand at a party with someone who was likely to be married to someone else back home. The physiotherapists did their best to keep this confidential for the female artist's reputation, but sometimes it came out. If I was aware of the situation, I brought the woman food and water at the hotel to help them recover in time to perform on the next tour stop.

Then there were the "tour bunnies," or Cirque groupies, who followed their favourite performers from city to city. The acrobats dropped them like flies and moved on to the next. I sometimes wondered if these male acrobats had "tour babies" all over America and didn't even know. I'm sure that was part of what drew me to Dominic. He wasn't a boy-child acrobat. He was a man. We didn't tell many people that we were together at first since he was so fresh from his breakup, plus to be honest, we liked the secrecy of dating with no one knowing. It was exciting, but he was also nervous about people judging him for dating a nineteen-year-old.

The sex antics were often fuelled by the drugs and alcohol that made frequent appearances on tour. I wouldn't say there was heavy opioid abuse, but by the end of 2005, after about six months on the road, the physiotherapists started to confiscate our painkillers. If you got injured and a doctor prescribed Vicodin or Percocet, as the tour progressed, it was either taken away or administered to you by the physiotherapist. At the time it was quite easy to get painkillers and performance-enhancing drugs when you saw a different doctor in every city, because everywhere we went the walk-in clinics loved

Cirque. There was a handful of artists who had pills for breakfast just to get through the pain from injuries and survive the gruelling schedule. It was this mix of factors that made the physiotherapists monitor the situation.

I didn't really understand the need for painkillers until I was performing in San Francisco and I injured my ankle. I had done a flip from bed to bed, landed and did a split leap, and didn't watch my landing. I was in so much shock. I knelt on the trampoline and my partner tried to help me to my feet because the act kept going, but I was frozen. The music was blaring and the audience was applauding, I kept saying, "I can't, I can't," over and over. It all happened so quickly, and I felt like throwing up. I had to be carried offstage.

My ankle felt disconnected from my entire foot, it was facing the other way and I was unable to move it. It was one of the worst pains I had ever experienced. I had lots of ankle sprains, constant pain in my back and joints, and that stupid turf toe, but never an ankle subluxation, which is when the tendons slip out of their normal position.

I was out of commission for two weeks with my ankle the size of a football, and I was on crutches. But I stayed on tour for my recovery. Typically, if an artist had an injury, they were sent back to Montreal to do their rehabilitation and were put on disability pay. It was a huge pay cut, and I didn't want to do that. I remained on tour and pushed through the pain and started to do my house tricks in the show to support the other acts. That way I still got paid my show fee. But I came back way too early, and my ankle was basically taped together because without it, I could barely walk. This happened a lot at Cirque. Artists wouldn't fully recover from an injury because they were losing money, so they made the comeback too early and relied on painkillers to get them through. It was my turn to rely heavily on painkillers and only then did I realize why the physiotherapists were monitoring the prescription medications so closely.

I couldn't get through a day without them. My cocktail of Tylenol 3 and Vicodin was what allowed me to survive and perform. But my stomach was in pieces after the damage of all those drugs. I began to eat less and lose weight, and just popped the pills. This was on top of my already compromised nutrition, or what I guess you could call an eating disorder.

After my wisdom tooth surgery, I lost ten pounds, so when I returned to Cirque, I was praised for my new physique. Clearly, the body complexes never ended for women in sport or entertainment, and I was as much a victim of it as any other girl. But Cirque took it to a whole other level. I was one of the "heavier" girls and I didn't like feeling that way. So, I began overexercising, ate only vegetables and fruit with ketchup for flavour, and didn't eat after three in the afternoon. Essentially, I returned to my gymnastics diet while doing ten shows per week. I developed a stomach ulcer. But I was back to weighing 112 pounds, and I started to receive positive attention for my weight loss and felt respected by my castmates. Yet, any health professional would say that for a five-foot-seven woman, that's too thin.

Years later, as I reflect on that period of my life, it's obvious that I had an unhealthy relationship with food. But there isn't much choice for women in the entertainment world. Especially when your body is your job. We have to look a certain way. Both to do the stunts needed, and to have that sexy, streamlined body that the audience finds desirable. It's a strange world. No one told me to diet; I just felt the pressure and knew I didn't fit in being the "heavy girl." But if you lost weight, you'd be praised for it. If you gained weight, you could hear people whispering under their breath.

Eventually, my ankle healed as best it could, but for the remainder of the tour, I taped both my ankles to prevent another subluxation. As the tour went on, moving from city to city, I performed and did my school work at night. I was counting down the days until I was done with my contract. It wasn't anything against Cirque or my fellow artists, I just couldn't do the same thing every day. It very quickly began to feel a lot like my years training as a gymnast. The same routine, day in, month out, and it wasn't what I had envisioned my adult life to be, no matter how much money I was making.

I soon finished my public relations education and received my certificate. I was so proud of myself for completing it in under a year. But I needed something else to distract me from the gruelling routine, and to have some say, some control, over my life. The group routines were a start, and I was grateful. But I knew that if I ever wanted to perform after *Corteo,* I needed to create a solo act.

I had grown close with a beautiful Russian girl named Anastasia, who was a tightrope walker. I'd watch her wow audiences every night with her solo routine. With the help of Anastasia and Lori, one of the technicians, we developed a solo aerial act for me. Despite being exhausted from that evening's performance, we stayed in the tent all hours of the night, flying in the air and working on my act, which was a combination of rhythmic gymnastics, contortion, and aerial. I wanted to tailor an act to my strengths and not continue to perform something that didn't fit my body technique and shape.

Lori spliced a rope with hand loops for me and I manipulated the rope on the floor, using my rhythmic gymnastics skills, as well as working the rope like a whip. Then I connected it to a swivel that lifted me up twenty to fifty feet in the air, where I did high-flying tricks on it. This solo aerial act made me feel like a bird. Yet, it was extremely painful, because it meant I hung from my neck, feet, one wrist, back, and hips, all of which meant I was left with deep rope burns every time. But it was all worth it. I was used to pain and eventually my body adapted. I guess that's why no one had an act like mine, because it was so damn painful hanging with all my weight on a skinny, unforgiving rope.

Behind the scenes the dramas continued as we neared the end of our two-and-a-half-year contract. Touring isn't for everyone. It's hard to explain to an outside person or partner why infidelity and adultery are so common on the road. But you put thirty beautiful acrobats together on a global tour for years with no rules, and a lot of them making money for the first time, it's no wonder that drugs, alcohol, and sex always made their way in. You were doing death-defying acts every night and trusting your partner to not let you fall, so unconventional bonds formed. Some performances were intimate acts that acrobats performed together day in and day out. It was like watching an intimate movie scene, and was why perhaps some actors dated their co-stars after they were done filming. Artists left their families, husbands, wives, friends, girlfriends, or boyfriends at home and embarked with a new family travelling the world. If you've ever heard about the Olympic Village being a cesspool for sex (they hand out condoms), you can imagine that Cirque du Soleil was the same or worse. But Cirque was our employer and provided an incredible opportunity for so many, including international acrobats, to have a better life, escape violence and poverty, and provide for their families back home. It was never Cirque's job to babysit us. It was on us to make our own choices. Choices we needed to live with. It's a lifestyle that no one can understand until they're in it.

I continued to develop my aerial act but didn't renew my contract on *Corteo*. After the incident with the fill-in acrobat who was under the influence of some substance, I vowed never again to perform in a group. *Corteo* didn't have a place for my solo act, and I still wasn't sure if I wanted to perform at all. I needed a change. Like all those years before when I gave up gymnastics to pursue other sports, I decided to quit performing. I left the tour, said good-bye to my Cirque family, and headed back home to Toronto, until eventually Montreal pulled me back in.

During my last few days on *Corteo* I met a woman by the name of Debra Brown. Cirque had brought her in to revamp the show and to light a fire under the artists, who were appearing sluggish on stage. Debra was an award-winning choreographer and had a unique style that inspired us and allowed us to feel free to experiment as we performed. She also had to work with my replacement and give the show some overall love after it had been on the road for two years. It's easy to lose the love of a show and grow bored when you've performed it over and over for two years.

After one performance Debra stayed back and caught me training my solo aerial act and just loved it. She encouraged me to be less of a "rhythmic gymnast" with the act and whip my hair around more and get more grounded and bend my knees. She wanted to shake the gymnast out of me and make me more soulful. She opened my eyes to a new style that I never knew I had in me. The more vulnerable, feminine, and sexy side. Debra pulled that right out of me in a few days before I left the tour. She saw something in me, she saw my heart, my hurt, and my soul, and she knew before I did that I wasn't done performing.

Debra and I stayed in touch after I left *Corteo* and returned to Toronto for a short time in 2007. I even tried moving to New York to see what the buzz was all about, but it wasn't for me. I didn't even last three months. I attempted to land a job in public relations, but entry-level roles came with a much lower salary than I was used to from performing, so I turned them down. I had grown accustomed to the money I'd made at Cirque and didn't want to step backward. I was struggling once again, searching for something that I couldn't find. I was lonely, lost, and confused, and I didn't know what my next move was.

During this time I sent Debra demos of my aerial act after I'd incorporated more of her suggestions. She loved it even more and invited me to Montreal to be a part of a show she was producing. It was a cabaret show called *Line 1* that was sexy, intimate, and had live music. It was the next challenge I was searching for and would be my next reinvention, what I consider my fifth life, that of a solo aerialist.

During our time together, Debra transformed me into a soloist and world-class performer. She took my aerial act and helped me own it. She changed my old gymnastics habits of presenting and posing and made me be simply me, only more so. She taught me to own my body, to breathe from my soul, and to reflect and embrace the audience. To make eye contact and just be in the moment, still, quiet, not moving, but with purpose. She was and still is a master of choreography. Debra was the angel I needed to transform who I was and give me confidence. I took the stage every night in her show with the other performers as Mary Sanders, the soloist, with no apologies. I owned the stage every night in six-inch heels and surprised many who knew me. They had never seen me in this sexy, female-empowered light. I was a new woman thanks to Debra. It probably also helped my new image that I cracked a whip during my act. Yes, a real whip, not like the thin rope I'd used during those post-show night practices at Cirque, this whip required me to wear glasses in order to not take an eye out. I had found my love of performing again. I knew the stage was what I longed for, it completed me.

We did a whole run of *Line 1* shows, and I got great feedback after my debut. Cirque du Soleil talent scouts were always present at shows like this, scouting their next hire, because Debra always thought so outside the box. Cirque knocked on my door again, but this time for an aerial contract. It was a resident show in Japan. I was invited to the workshop to test out the bungee equipment act that I'd be part of if I accepted the contract. I liked it; it was fun, but it wasn't my act. It was a group bungee act. While I liked the feeling of flying and bungee jumping over and over, I turned it down. I didn't want to uproot my life for an act I wasn't crazy about and move to Japan. I'd learned my lessons during those tough two and a half years on *Corteo,* I was no longer the naive nineteen-year-old fresh off the Olympics who was willing to do anything anyone told me. Things were different now. I was different. If I were to hit the road again, it would be for the right act in the right show.

Cirque came knocking again halfway through 2008, and this time it was for their show *Delirium.* What set *Delirium* apart from *Corteo* was the venues. *Delirium* was an arena show, not a tent show. Arena shows were a completely different ball game. You had changing rooms and tour buses, and the crowds were four times the size of tent shows. I was tapped for *Delirium* after a rhythmic artist didn't return following one of their breaks and they needed an immediate replacement. It proved to be a new experience all around. Not only was it performed in arenas and stadiums, but it was also a European tour that involved only five to seven shows per week, less than we did on *Corteo.* It also meant jumping on a tour bus and sleeping in your bunk throughout the night, waking up in a new city or country and performing for a brand-new audience. It was more of the rockstar life like the Tour of Champions, and I jumped at it.

By this point I had also I moved in with Dominic. He had shared custody of his daughter and she stayed with us on and off. I was still only twenty-two, and being around a child 50 percent of the time who was not yet five years old was a huge culture shock to me. I wasn't prepared to be a "mom" to anyone. *Delirium* gave the relationship some space, and gave me time to consider whether Dominic, and becoming a stepmom, was what I wanted.

My role in *Delirium* was the *Chaman* character, who is a healer and someone who can enter the world of the unconscious. Or at least, that's what I was told. Regardless, the role involved me doing rhythmic gymnastics and being a main solo character, and my aerial act was a backup number for the show. Backup numbers were often used when another act was out due to injury, which happened a lot. I was excited to debut my act on Cirque's world stage. Solo characters were also paid very well. I was pumped. I had signed a deal to do what I was good at, rhythmic gymnastics, be a main character, and perform and train my aerial act. I couldn't ask for anything more. I said goodbye to Dominic and his daughter, and I packed my bags and headed to Europe.

When I arrived I could tell immediately that the *Delirium* tour was going to be different. For starters, I was picked up at the airport and taken to a five-star hotel. This was a real change from the kind of lower-budget hotels where we stayed on tour with *Corteo*. I hadn't often experienced upscale treatment in my life, if ever, and I'm not going to lie — I loved it.

The cast of *Delirium* was also incredible. It was highly dance focused and a few of the dancers were from Toronto. I meshed with these young women almost immediately and they became my core group. As you know, feeling a sense of belonging is something I've always wanted, but often didn't have. So the fact that, for once, I wasn't the outsider made the *Delirium* experience all the better.

In addition to dancers, the show had singers, drummers, and other musicians who performed on stage right beside you in the action. I had loved live music since my time at *Line 1* with Debra. Having the musicians so close to you gave you more passion, and you felt more at one with everyone around you.

I also loved my costume and makeup for this show. My costume was a skin-tight sheer mesh bodysuit with red paint and swirls in the appropriate areas to cover up my private parts. I had long blond horse-like hair extensions that the costume person wove into my natural hair every night. These extensions also matched a tail on the costume. Granted, it damaged my hair immensely, but I still loved the look. Putting on my makeup was a very long process, as is the norm for Cirque. It was mainly red makeup to match the paint on my sheer unitard, with lots of swirls and one line down the centre of my nose, mouth, and chin all the way to my neck. Then for the neck part, it was with my sheer costume, so it all looked like one unified piece of art. All in all, it took over two hours to perfect.

The performer who had originated the *Chaman* had chosen the ball as the main apparatus for her act. I chose to follow in her foot-steps and rolled the ball and balanced it in contortion-like moves. Performing and competing were two very different things. The crowd went wild for skills that judges wouldn't even blink an eye at. I learned early on in my gymnastics touring days that I didn't need to do the toughest skills and risk making errors, I only needed those that seemed very impressive to the untrained eye. For example, I stood and placed the ball on my head, lifted my right leg above my head, and held it with only my foot. It was a crowd-pleaser every time. But for Olympic judges, not so much.

My solo character and contortion act was going well, but I con-tinued working on my aerial act. Interestingly, Lori, the technician who helped me create my act on *Corteo,* was also on *Delirium* and he continued flying me after shows. All the work proved timely because one night a Chinese acrobat who performed an aerial duo strap act got injured and the producers needed to fill their three-minute number. The duo strap was an apparatus that was two long pieces of material about eight feet long with no stretch in them. The artists hung from them, typically only with their hands, and held on to one another and flew in all sorts of directions. It was a popular act at Cirque and appeared in numerous shows. The Chinese artist's misfortune was my chance to showcase my own solo rope act in front of a live audience. I modified my existing routine to the music and length of the Chinese act. As a backup act, you need to be able to adapt your act to different music or styles. The concept of their number was a "battle" where one aerialist wore red and the other wore blue. It was a fight between the two sides, with musicians and dancers below them also duking it out through dance and music that consisted solely of drumming and was very fast-paced. The drummers battled each other on both ends of the stage and the aerialists flew in the middle. It was intense, and I loved it. I accepted the challenge, got fitted for my costume, which consisted of tights and a bra, all very superhero, and was off to war.

I was very nervous because I didn't have much time to prepare or choreograph my routine to the new music, but Lori helped me out. That was the thing about replacement acts, you rarely had twenty-four hours before you went live, so I needed to be ready to modify my act and its style to fit in the show where needed on short notice. The act went off without a hitch. The crowd loved it. It was highly contortion-based with fewer death-defying, risky skills, but I continued to work at it after that night, eventually becoming a regular alternate in the show to give the duo strap artists a break.

Shortly after this, another solo artist who had a six-minute number had a tragedy occur in his family and he had to fly back home to Russia. It was abrupt. He found out the morning of a show day that his father had passed. He immediately left the arena, and I only had a few hours to extend my act from a three-minute number to a six-minute number. I integrated more floor work to help offset the time in the air. I worked very hard with Lori to get ready to go on. I performed the act in my *Chaman* costume because it was so close together with my other contortion act that I didn't have time to change. But I liked that I was recognizable throughout a large portion of the show.

This longer act went well, the crowd accepted it with generous applause. It was a proud moment for me in my performance career, and one that I have on my website as a keepsake. I wish I'd had more time to perfect the act in that form, since I loved the music and style. It had a slower, sexier vibe as opposed to the drumming battle from the shorter routine. However, the soloist who lost his father returned quickly and took the stage. His first show back had us all in tears. He was shaking throughout the entire act as he dedicated it to his father and was holding back tears the entire time. It was one of the most touching and emotional performances I have seen to this day. His dad was definitely there with him, holding him up throughout his routine, and I'm sure was very proud of him.

We had more time off on *Delirium* than any show I had ever done. Sometimes we only did three shows per week depending on the tour schedule. We were paid a weekly salary plus per diem, regardless of how many shows we did. It was a lot better than being paid per show. I really liked this structure and stability. I was still quite cautious with money, since I was always saving. *Delirium* was only going to be an eight-month tour, and it was uncertain if it would continue because it had already been touring for many years, so I wanted to have some financial security when the tour was done. I never relied on Dominic or anyone for money, I always strived to be self-sufficient, having learned the hard way by watching my mother struggle. I didn't want to struggle financially if I could avoid it.

We couldn't always travel city to city on the buses because sometimes our next show was too far away. In these instances we flew to the next location and had a few days off, because the crew needed to bus in with the equipment. I sometimes felt bad for the technicians and crew on *Delirium*, as I had with *Corteo*. Here we were getting to jump on a plane and enjoy time off in the most beautiful cities around the world, and they had to pile into buses for long rides to get to the next town. But none of them complained. As I keep saying, the technicians were truly the silent stars of our shows.

Throughout *Delirium* my mother remained a constant in my life. Matt and Mike were busy at university achieving straight As or just about starting their careers. She was still working three jobs, trying her best to make ends meet and help support my brothers' tuition debts, among other things. Other things being Rick's wine habit and lack of ability to keep a job. I tried to help when I could, but I was also saving up so I could support myself when I eventually got off the road. Despite the money woes, my mother managed to visit me in Paris. It was the highlight of my tour. We loved roaming the streets of Paris together. We went to the Louvre and saw the *Mona Lisa* and visited other museums (although we typically just went straight for the bar after an hour or so to catch up and talk). My mom stayed with me in my room, and we indulged in room service and lounged in our robes. The hair and makeup person made my mom into a circus performer before one of our shows. She dolled her up and added hair extensions similar to what I wore each night. She rocked a red streak in her blond bob very well. I get tears in my eyes remembering my mom cheering away in the audience with that red streak in her hair. She sang along and enjoyed every moment of it. She was my biggest supporter, best friend, and the sister I never had. It was the saddest moment of the tour when I had to say goodbye to her and move on to the next city. I remember boarding the bus, putting her in a taxi to move to a hotel closer to the airport, and driving off. I was worried seeing her drive off in a foreign country into the dark, but nothing could ever stop my mom. She is fearless and made it home safely.

I wished she could have stayed on the road with me, but we weren't allowed family members, since there were limited bunks on each bus. If one person could have family with them, then everyone would want someone with them. It wasn't fair to the rest of the cast, let alone legal, to have too many people on the tour buses. I remember back in 2004 on the gymnastics tour, we had family or friends ride with us from city to city, but those were only for the short hauls that didn't require people to have bunks to sleep in. In Europe it was a different story. The rides were longer, and we needed our sleep to be able to wake up and perform the next day.

Like during my *Corteo* days, the *Delirium* tour had its share of drama, unconventional relationships, and controversy. But I was older and wasn't as shocked by it as I had been on *Corteo*. Relationships between technicians and artists were more prominent on this tour. Many continued off tour and couples went on to get married and have kids. It was nice to see, and pretty rare. But in my case, distance didn't make the heart grow fonder, and Dominic and I grew apart. I didn't miss him like I had on *Corteo*. Perhaps because I had more friends and felt like part of the tour family on *Delirium*.

There was one person in particular that I grew close to. His name was Victor, he was an acrobat from Ukraine. And by close, I mean "close," if you get my drift. It was very hard to draw the line between friends and more than friends with Victor. It didn't help that Victor performed essentially in a Speedo every night and was one of the fittest people I'd ever met. He was also protective of me, and I liked it. I never really had a male figure look out for me the way he did, not even Dominic. Victor was old school, and really treated me like a princess. Even when my mom came to visit, he sent flowers and champagne to our room for no reason. He was a true gentleman and never expected anything in return. Everyone on tour knew we had a thing for each other. Touring is lonely, and I was lonely on *Corteo* watching everyone around me with someone, I guess I didn't want to be alone on this tour. Against my better judgment, I became like the performers I'd judged harshly on *Delirium* and *Corteo*. Though deep down I think I knew that Dominic wasn't the one for me. I just couldn't face the truth of it.

Dominic visited once during my eight-month contract. I could tell he knew I was losing interest. Victor kept his distance when Dominic visited. But Dominic knew some of the technicians on the tour and I assumed they told him I was spending a lot of time with Victor. I remember when we returned from dinner when he was visiting, we went up in the elevator and when the doors opened, there was Victor. I just froze, but it also happened to be Victor's birthday that day. I wished him happy birthday in front of Dominic (pretty bold move, I guess) and he smiled and said thanks to me. Then Dominic also wished him an insincere happy birthday. I could feel in that moment that Dominic knew there was something between Victor and me. He never said anything, though. I couldn't wait for Dominic to go back to Montreal. He just didn't belong in the *Delirium* tour bubble. He knew I felt this way and had something up his sleeve for when I returned home for the holidays.

The holiday season found me and Dominic and my family skating at Toronto's Nathan Phillips Square. I was in a thin leather jacket, leggings, and ice skates. First, I don't like winter or winter sports; and second, I didn't know how to skate, so you can imagine my state of mind in that moment. Dominic was exceptional at ice skating since he used to play hockey; he was having the time of his life. However, I was hating every minute of it and couldn't wait for it to be over. At a certain point, I admitted defeat. I was too cold and wanted those skates off my weak ankles. We headed inside to the change area to warm up and take the skates off. Before I knew it, I was on the floor. I had blacked out. I guess from not eating enough (I remember only having some chocolate for lunch that day), or perhaps the contrast between cold to hot, I just collapsed. But as I recovered and looked around at my family, it occurred to me that perhaps there was a point to all this. At that moment I realized he was going to propose at some point that day and my family was in on it.

We headed back to Mom and Rick's place. They were renting a pretty swanky condo in a building called "Palace Pier" in Etobicoke after they were forced to sell the townhouse. It was a beautiful complex with extremely high maintenance fees. They were still living beyond their means in a two-bedroom condo with a water view because Rick still couldn't get his "shit" together. But Rick would never live in a "cheap" place. As a salesman he always needed to save face.

Once we arrived back at their home, I had a splitting headache and was still digesting what the hell just happened. Why did I black out? Was I subconsciously foreshadowing what was about to happen and my body just knew to shut down? Did my body know it was wrong before I did? Who knows. Someone handed me a cosmopolitan, since it was my favourite drink at the time, and we sat around eating and drinking. But I still didn't feel right, so Dominic and I headed downstairs to the guest quarters in the building. I went to bed. But Dominic wouldn't settle, he just tossed and turned. Next thing I knew, he was on his knee with a ring. Yup. He got up in the middle of the night to propose. All I wanted to do was sleep. Not exactly romantic. My immediate reaction was WTF. I was so utterly confused and had conflicting emotions, but I said yes because he seemed so sad and missed me while I was away (while I was missing Victor), and I still had another two months of the tour to finish.

The next morning we had brunch, and all laughed about the fact that the plan was for Dominic to propose in the middle of Nathan Phillips Square, but I was too cold and ruined the entire event. Well, that should have been a sign right there. Clearly, he didn't know me well enough not to plan a proposal in the freezing cold on ice. Oh well. The engagement happened and I was ready to move on. We returned home to Montreal and the wedding was set for spring 2009.

It was an extremely confusing time. I didn't wear my engagement ring when I returned to the *Delirium* tour, mostly because I couldn't on stage for safety reasons, but also out of pure confusion about how I felt about it all. I never told Victor I'd gotten engaged either.

As the tour drew to a close, we all kept hoping it would get extended, but it never did. I was sad to hear the news because it truly was a beautiful show. We just ran out of arenas to play. The tour had already passed through North America before I had joined. However, they did film our last few shows and released it in movie theaters nationwide. Being able to rewatch *Delirium* in my living room never gets old for me. I never got to see it in theaters because it aired while we were still on the road, but I made sure to secure a DVD to show my children one day.

*Delirium* gave me the best eight months of my performance career to date. I cried at the end; we all did. I said goodbye to Victor, which broke my heart. *Delirium* was also a wrap for my Cirque du Soleil touring days. It was now time to return to the real world and all that I knew was waiting for me.

One thing that was waiting for me was a letter informing me that I had been inducted into the USA Gymnastics Hall of Fame. It was an incredible honour to join my father in the Hall of Fame. My life had truly come full circle. Many members of my family joined me for the incredible ceremony where they played videos of my career, and many who had known my dad were in attendance. They were very happy to see that Fred's "little Olympian" had achieved Olympian status. It was a very emotional night and I have the most beautiful plaque to show for it that now hangs in my office. Not long after my Hall of Fame induction, I received a letter from the World Olympians Association. It was a Certificate of Recognition for my achievement as an Olympian that granted use of the post-nominal letters, OLY, to my name to signify my ongoing role in society as an Olympian living and promoting the Olympic values. From here on out, my name would read, Mary Sanders, OLY. It was very cool, and I also have this certificate hanging in my office to remind myself daily of the important role I play in society as an Olympian.

O

As for Dominic, I had doubts about our ability to be happy, but I was so far down the path to marriage I couldn't turn back. I was very lost after *Delirium*, so I went with what was safe — which was a life with Dominic — and hoped he would change and put me first and we would live happily ever after. And when I first came home from *Delirium*, he had missed me so much he cried and was nice and romantic.

Ultimately, I think it was out of pity that I said yes to him. But once our wedding was around the corner, Dominic's niceness and romantic gestures disappeared, and it was his daughter first and I was an afterthought. It was as though he was confident that he had me for good, so he didn't have to make any more effort. I think he knew I wouldn't call off the wedding because I was afraid of embarrassment or failure (and losing all that deposit money!). There is also the spectre of the daddy issues in my life — stability and kind, trustworthy men were very hard to come by in my upbringing, which played a role in why I married Dominic. I truly wanted not to have an unhappy marriage. I was so young, and Dominic seemed the polar opposite of my stepfathers. Added to that, he was older, which gave me the sense of security I craved. I promised myself that if I married him, I'd never leave him, because I didn't want to go down the path of multiple husbands.

Dominic and I were married in May of 2009. We had about 120 people at the wedding, including close friends and family, mostly from Toronto and Montreal. On the morning of the wedding, there was the biggest hailstorm I had ever witnessed. I was late to the ceremony because of it. The pellets were the size of golf balls, and as I sat there in my dress waiting for the storm to subside, I couldn't help but think, perhaps it was a sign from God. Was he literally throwing the biggest storm my way to prevent me from marrying Dominic? It may very well have been God's plan to make me miss the wedding, but somehow, I made it to the altar. I knew people were waiting and I worried more about them than my own feelings at this point.

Dominic's family primarily spoke French, so I'm not sure how much of the wedding they understood, since most of the speeches were in English. There was also a lot of tension at this point with Dominic's daughter in the picture. Dominic was having her live with us more and more. He and his ex were fighting over custody and who would spend more time with her. Granted, I was young and wanted more time with Dominic, so there was this constant battle about who got more of Dominic's time, me or his daughter. I loved his daughter very much and she holds a special place in my heart, but being in my early twenties, I needed more than what I was receiving. Between work, travel, and minimal time at home, it was often shared with Dominic's daughter. I didn't feel that I was put first, unlike how Victor had made me feel, and deep down I knew that's what I wanted from a relationship.

Before we got married, we had a huge fight about whether his daughter would be at the wedding. For once I wanted it to be just us to celebrate with our families. Of course, Dominic wanted his daughter to be the flower girl and to dance the night away with us all. He didn't even want to get a babysitter; he wanted her there with us the entire night. I can see where he was coming from, having guilt about leaving his ex-girlfriend and never wanting his daughter to feel left out, but I knew the wedding would not feel like it was to celebrate us; instead, it was to celebrate as a family with his daughter. I don't know why, but I just wasn't happy with that decision. Call me selfish, but I just wasn't happy sharing my special day with his daughter. But she did come to the wedding and was a flower girl. Dominic's mother looked after her and took her back to her hotel at the end of the evening. From that point forward, we were rarely just the two of us; we always shared our time with his daughter.

I leaned into my Christian faith to get through and accept this. the Bible says to put God first, then your spouse, and then your children. I assume it is because if you are not one with your partner, your children will suffer. The Bible also says that when we get married, we become one flesh.

"For this reason a man will leave his father and mother and be united to his wife, and the two will become one flesh. So they are no longer two, but one flesh. Therefore what God has joined together, let no one separate" (Mark 10:7–9).

But in my heart, I didn't feel that Dominic and I were one flesh. We were growing apart, struggling to spend time as a couple between travels and home life. I knew I wasn't happy, but I would never be the one to break a marriage. In sickness and in health, right? So, no matter how unhappy and unappreciated I was, I would stick it out. And now that *Delirium* was over, what I would do next was a giant question mark. It was time to reinvent once again.

## What I Learned

**Reason:** My reason to get out of bed was the joy of learning to come out of my shell and develop into a confident, female-empowered solo performer.

**Reinvent:** The transition needed to happen from being a group performer in *Corteo*, into being the solo aerialist I dreamed of being. But sometimes reinvention comes in steps, and from Life Four to Five, that's what happened. Life Four, an acrobat, needed to unfold as it did, or I couldn't have gone from the Olympics to being the woman in *Delirium*. And that's what you need to know about reinvention. Sometimes it's a clear and even abrupt change, at other times it's a slow evolution. There is no right or wrong way to reinvent yourself, just listen to the signs.

**Right:** It was my right to push away from the structure that Cirque gave and challenge myself to try new things. It's easy to stay in your comfort zone, and many people who love you will tell you to stay the course, stability is the be all and end all. But it is your life, and that gives you the right to decide when stability is what you need, or if you crave a change.

O

Life Five, Mary the soloist, would continue, but it would evolve into Life Six ...

With my father, Fred, during our time living on Salt Spring Island, circa 1989.

On Salt Spring Island with my mother, Jaci, and my two brothers, Mike (far left) and Matt (wearing yellow), circa 1988.

My first-ever rhythmic gymnastics photo wearing a leotard my mother made me, circa 1995.

Showing the moves that got me crowned Canadian Junior National Champion in 1998.

## Local Rhythmic Gymnast Wins Gold

Mary Sanders, a Grade 7 student at Bliss Carmen School, recently placed first overall in the Junior Level, 1998 Elite Canada Gymnastic Competition. In the individual events Mary won 3 gold medals and one silver.

Following the competition, Mary competed at the international level in France and placed second overall. Mary is thankful for the support and prayers of family and friends. Mary trains at Kalev Rhythmic Club in North York.

An article in the local newspaper after I returned from France having placed second in a prestigious junior competition, where I first made a name for myself on the international stage.

Crowned Canadian National Champion in 2002, my first Canadian title.

Reaching for my clubs while performing a split leap during the 2003 World Championships. (Courtesy of the estate of Patrick Tower.)

Ready to hit the mat to perform with the hoop, my highest scoring routine, as my coach, Mimi Masleva, looks on during the World Championships in 2003.

In the kiss-and-cry zone
with Mimi following one
of my routines in 2003.
(Courtesy of Louis Pereira.)

Practicing in the warm-up
area with my clubs and getting last minute advice from
Mimi at a 2003 competi-
tion. (Courtesy of Louis Pereira.)

Catching the hoop under my leg as I perform a split leap during the 2004 U.S. Olympic
Trials. (Copyright Jonathan Ferrey/Getty Images.)

Flying high during the U.S. Olympic Trials in 2004 in San Jose, California. (Copyright Jonathan Ferrey/Getty Images.)

Waving to the crowd as they announce my name as winner of the Olympic Trials in 2004. (Copyright Jeff Gross/Getty Images.)

It's official! I earned my Olympic berth by winning the U.S. Olympic Trials in 2004.
(Copyright Jeff Gross/Getty Images.)

Taking part in my first professional photo shoot for *Vanity Fair*'s Special Collectors' Edition: "The Olympians," 2004. (Copyright Bruce Weber.)

Performing the dance portion of my ribbon routine during the 2004 Olympics in Athens. (Courtesy of the estate of Patrick Tower.)

A final fist-pump as I successfully complete my last routine. I went four for four clean routines on the Olympic stage. (Courtesy of the estate of Patrick Tower.)

# The gymnast who leapt over the moon

## The star of Cirque du Soleil by Abbot Prince Street

CALL MARY SANDERS an Ambassador of North York, call her a Homecoming Queen, call her Someone Who Makes a Living Jumping Up and Down on a Bed in Cirque du Soleil, but whatever you do ... don't call her lazy.

"I started training when I was born because my dad was my coach," Sanders says in the performers' tent at Cirque du Soleil in Ontario Place. As performers stretch into positions unknown to most mortals, she recounts growing up as a child prodigy.

Sanders's family moved to British Columbia shortly after she was born in North York General Hospital. At the age of seven, she returned home and continued training under her father's (renowned American Olympic gymnast Fred Sanders) tutelage.

He passed away a few years later, and she was forced to switch from standard gymnastics to a more rhythmic kind, due to a growth spurt, but she remained undaunted. With a new coach, she attended York Mills Collegiate Institute and began competing.

"I liked it, but I wasn't there very much," she says. "Out of a month, I'd be there a week and a half."

Winning championships across Canada while her peers spent time studying for the driving test made for a unique, if not scattered, York Mills High School career.

"School was tough, but I had teachers who really supported me as an athlete and helped me get to where I am today," she says.

Sanders went on to become junior champion and two-time senior champion of Canada.

"I started competing for the U.S. because I wanted to follow along my father's footsteps. The U.S. supported me all the way through — financially and emotionally."

In America, she went on to win

the nationals three times and qualified for the 2004 Summer Olympics. But the thrill of returning home is palpable when she describes the long-missed friends and family who have seen her during her current Cirque du Soleil Canadian tour.

"It's always been my dream to join Cirque du Soleil," she says.

So far, Sanders has played Montreal, Quebec and now Toronto with the high-flying show then, later this month, she'll be returning to the States. She plans on going to university for broadcast journalism,

but for now she simply says, "I'm grateful to be here."

The pressures inherent in leading a teenage double life required a delicate touch in the fickle world of high school politics, Sanders explains. When asked if she enjoyed the social atmosphere at York Mills, she laughs, declaring, "I put my career first and kept to myself and my sport. After the Olympics, when I came home, I ran into some people from my class, and they said, 'So, that's what you were doing!'" This month, classmates will have a chance to see her again.

### REPORT CARD

**STUDENT** Mary Sanders **GRADUATED** York Mills
**BEST SUBJECT** Business **WORST SUBJECT** English
**CURRENT JOB** Performer, Cirque du Soleil

A news clipping from 2008 about me as the local girl who joined Cirque du Soleil.

Playing an angel during Cirque du Soleil's *Corteo* in 2005. (Courtesy of Lóránt Vörös.)

Backstage with my mom at Cirque du Soleil's *Delirium* in Paris in 2008.

Portraying the *Chaman* during a transition number for Cirque du Soleil's *Delirium* in 2008. (Courtesy of Lóránt Vörös.)

One of my favourite makeup designs from Cirque du Soleil for one of the company's special events in 2013. (Courtesy of Spencer Xiong.)

Showing my stripes as my Cirque du Soleil zebra character as part of special events for the company in 2012. (Courtesy of Spencer Xiong.)

Working the straps during the finale of the post-Olympics gymnastics tour during the fall of 2016. (Courtesy of John Cheng.)

Hanging by my feet for the last move of the silk routine during the 2016 post-Olympics gymnastics tour. (Courtesy of John Cheng.)

Performing the same move from which I fell almost to my death weeks earlier during the 2016 post-Olympics gymnastics tour. (Courtesy of John Cheng.)

There's a new "shark" in town. Sitting on the *Shark Tank* set at Sony Studios in Culver City, California, in 2015.

Performing my surprise ribbon dance for my new husband at our wedding in 2018.
(Courtesy of Adam Biesenthal Photography.)

My husband, David, holding our son, Gabriel, and in my arms, my daughter, Ava, during the pandemic in September 2020. (Courtesy of Boy Girl Photography Studio Ltd.)

On set for my first acting role as sports commentator Brianna Alcroft in *Olympians at Heart*, April 2021.
(Courtesy of Brain Power Studio.)

# 6<sup>TH</sup> LIFE:

# CREATIVE DIRECTOR & CHOREOGRAPHER

Winter 2012. I pour myself a glass of wine because my heart is beating uncontrollably. Dominic, his daughter, and I are gathered around the television, pretending to be a family for the sake of the child. While they sit on the sofa not five feet away, I am on our shared laptop and log into his Skype account. We have never been secretive about passwords, so this is a no-brainer. I scroll and find all his messages are to the same woman. Multiple calls, messages on messages between the two of them. She is his boss's assistant, which means that, as I suspected, he met her in Vancouver and then they were reunited in Doha. She is Australian and her name is Meredith. She is also married. They both complain about their spouses. His mistress writes, "I miss you, it's so hard to be apart. I will leave him soon so we can be together." And my husband responds, "It's so hard to be in the same house with her when all I want to do is be in the basement talking to you." It always ends with "I love you." This is the proof I need. I am hot with rage, but before I react, I need to screenshot, and copy and paste everything. I do this and send it all to my lawyer and ask if it is enough. Mercifully she responds immediately, saying, "You did it. I will draw up the papers." I feel as though the world has been lifted off my shoulders.

O

Three years earlier. Montreal, 2009. Before my sixth life was to begin, my personal life started to fall apart. And that was to be another hard lesson, that no matter how much you want something to work out, you can't control everything in life, particularly not another person's emotions. Up until this point, I had been able to focus on a goal and, with hard work, achieve my dreams: the Olympics, Cirque du Soleil, soaring high as a solo aerialist. But the same focus and determination that served me well as an athlete and performer didn't yield the same success in my marriage.

I was trying to be a good wife and partner to Dominic. Even though I'd had doubts about us, I wanted to make our marriage work. I'd seen my mother go through too much with her three husbands and I didn't want the same for me. At first things seemed fine between us. But settling into life in Montreal, and not touring all the time, was an adjustment for me. I needed to do something creative and earn money.

The answer was becoming an on-call performer in Cirque's special events department. This was a glamorous freelance gig where, with a collection of different performers, we put on a one- to two-hour show with a few days' notice. We all brought our talents and specialties to create magic on stage. Typically, it was only veteran performers who did special events because there was no room for error and we didn't have a lot of rehearsal time. These assignments brought me close to global billionaires and luminaries such as the

Prince of Dubai, the Entrepreneur of the Year in Monaco, and executives from Coca Cola, top financial institutions like Ernst & Young, Infiniti, Reebok, Bombardier, and many more. But it meant that Cirque could call you up any given day and you had to be ready.

I worked steadily in special events throughout 2009 to 2012. I loved this job because every event was different. I often crossed paths with people I'd worked with before, during the gymnastics tour or *Corteo*, and sometimes even Victor. Working closely with him on these occasions stirred old feelings in me because truth be known, I always thought of him as the one that got away. Realistically, we would never have had a future. Two people from opposite ends of the earth, it just wasn't meant to be. These special event trips were never longer than a few days, but our reunions were always incredible. We were never intimate again because I took my marriage vows seriously, but we reminisced and spent time together. It made me miss him all over again.

During this period I was invited to take part in the 2010 Olympic Winter Games as aerial captain and as a performer for the opening and closing ceremonies. Dominic was going to be on the technical team, so it was an amazing opportunity for us to leave Montreal and spend some time in a new city, just the two of us. The Winter Olympics were in Vancouver. It was surreal for me to participate in another Olympic event, especially in British Columbia, where I'd lived as a child and begun my gymnastic career with my father coaching me. The memories of those early days, and of him, came flooding back, as did the grief and feelings of immense loss.

Dominic and I lived in Vancouver for the next three months while his daughter stayed in Montreal. But we hardly saw each other. While I was training all day, he stayed after rehearsals to correct the technical equipment. We didn't get to go on dates or enjoy our time together in B.C. I was alone during most of my time off or hanging out with other cast members. Dominic spent a lot of time with his new boss, their assistants, and other technical staff. My gut told me things weren't moving in the right direction between us. My gut would prove right yet again. But I still clung to hope and the commitment I'd made to my marriage, which didn't keep me from getting jealous of the young women on the technical staff that he was spending so much time with.

Being a part of the opening and closing ceremonies of the Olympic Games was incredible, it brought back all my own memories from Athens six years prior. As aerial captain, I worked with an extensive team of choreographers, stage managers, directors, and about fifty aerialists. For our part of the opening ceremonies, we appeared to be skiers and snowboarders performing various tricks as we raced down the mountains that were projected on screens behind us. The timing had to be exact, if you were off by even a second, it jeopardized the entire performance. It was visually very powerful, although I'll admit now that it was also terrifying because it involved being suspended two hundred feet above ground with snowboards or skis on our feet fifteen minutes before we made our entrance. Being suspended in a harness for any period is painful, but add another ten to fifteen pounds for the snowboard and skis and it quickly became torture. Not that I could act terrified, since I was the captain. But it was the highest I had ever flown in a harness. Suffice it to say it was very challenging, given the amount of broken blood vessels and nerve damage we endured in our private areas from the harnesses. There were men doing this act as well, and they had some semi-permanent damage down under for quite some time after the Games. No pain, no gain, right?

The entirety of the opening ceremonies was amazing, but a major glitch happened during the lighting of the Olympic cauldron. One of the four arms that were to rise out of the snow to create the cauldron got stuck underground, which left torchbearer and Olympic gold medal speed skater Catriona Le May Doan standing with her torch as her co-torchbearers, hockey icon Wayne Gretzky, gold medal skier Nancy Greene, and basketball star Steve Nash, lit the other three. It was a bit of a *womp womp* moment, but that's live performance. Dominic was in charge of the cauldron, so he was very distraught.

I was also aerial captain for the closing ceremonies, but it was a much smaller act. I simply danced around as a maple leaf in the air and looked pretty. Super easy. Dominic and his team also created a wonderful Canadian humour moment where Le May Doan got to light an indoor cauldron after clown and mime Yves Dagenais appeared to solve the problem himself and the arm raised. It was hilarious and a great way to circle back and fix the glitch.

The Vancouver Games took place in February, and I enjoyed hanging around the Olympics once more, watching the events and feeling that Olympic buzz all over again. The fact that it was in Canada was also special, and that the national team went on to perform so well with twenty-six medals overall, and win fourteen gold, the highest number of gold medals of any nation. Given it was so close to Los Angeles, there was a large influx of Canadian celebrities on hand. Bryan Adams and K.D. Lang and others performed during the opening ceremonies, and Michael J. Fox, Ryan Reynolds, William Shatner, and of course Wayne Gretzky, were there too.

Being in B.C. also gave me the opportunity to visit my father's grave on Salt Spring Island. My mom and Rick, who had come to visit, also came with me. Dominic was working, so he didn't join us. He should have made the time to come with me to see where my father had passed, but perhaps that was another sign of the state of our marriage.

Salt Spring seemed different to me as an adult. Everything seemed smaller. It was very commercialized, and it didn't feel like the tiny island I grew up on. My father's gravesite was overgrown, and I couldn't even see the beautiful flowers or white cobblestone my mother had laid in his honour. I could barely even see his nameplate. It was sad, but his soul was in heaven and that's what mattered. I knocked on the door of our big blue house that didn't seem so big in my eyes anymore. The owners were gracious, kind, and remembered me. They took me on a tour of the home, which brought back all kinds of memories. Especially those stairs I used to sprain my ankle on and the attic where my brothers and I would have pillow and teddy bear fights.

After the Games were over, I returned to Montreal with Dominic and continued working for Cirque. I worked shows performing as a zebra, nymph, shaman, clown, fairy, and all sorts of characters. I wasn't doing solo acts; I was often just a character doing contortion. It was fun but not fulfilling.

As for my marriage, Dominic and I carried on. He left Cirque du Soleil after more than ten years to do the Vancouver Olympics contract. It was a big step for him, since he had had job security for so long. Now he was in the same freelancing boat as me. He didn't work for quite some time after Vancouver and started to worry. I was busier than ever doing the special events, but was also looking for my next big gig. We spent lots of time with his daughter, since we'd been gone for three months in Vancouver. But despite all this togetherness, we grew further and further apart. He was convinced that I didn't love his daughter and insisted that I had to prove otherwise by accepting her in our lives on a daily basis. I constantly let Dominic know that if he put me first on occasion there wouldn't be this tension. I even attempted counselling but that was a failure. Nothing resonated with him. He didn't comprehend that hiring a babysitter so that just the two of us could go out on a "date night" would be a good thing. Hiring a babysitter meant he was neglecting his daughter and he just wouldn't do it.

Looking back, I can see that I was selfish at times. I truly loved his daughter and did all sorts of gymnastics and other fun activities with her. I think it was my age that was the problem. Dominic was older and in a different place, and I was in my mid-twenties, wanting to feel loved and be treated like a princess and live in a fairy tale. Well, it wasn't a fairy tale marriage, that's for sure. I always felt I came last. Constantly asking for love and attention from your partner is a horrible feeling. And sharing love was not something I had ever experienced. It is such a hard thing to juggle stepchildren, especially if you're not mentally ready. Do I admit that I was jealous of his daughter at times? One hundred percent. Was I ready to be a stepmom? No. Now that I have two kids of my own, I know I would never let anyone stand in the way of time with my kids.

Eventually, Dominic got another contract with the same production company that put on the Vancouver Olympics. Except this time, it was for the 12th Pan Arab Games that took place in Doha, Qatar, from December 6 to 23, 2011. Dominic left in October and returned for a few days here and there. During these brief visits, he divided his time between his daughter and me, but he was always exhausted and jet-lagged. The plan was for him to be home for Christmas following the event, then we'd travel with his daughter to Winnipeg to spend the holiday with his family.

But over this three-month period, we grew further apart. We set up times to speak on video chats, but he often pushed our virtual dates aside, saying he was too busy working. I knew he was hanging out with the same group of people from the Vancouver Games who had made me jealous before, so I wasn't feeling very good about his behaviour. When I caught him on a video call, he wasn't wearing his wedding ring. When I asked why, he just said he forgot, or he couldn't wear it around the machinery. I knew it was all a lie, he never got his hands dirty. I had a feeling he had met someone. I never wanted to be fooled by anyone or feel vulnerable, nor did I want to compromise the financial security that I'd worked so hard for. Fearing the worst for my marriage, I met with a lawyer to get legal advice in case things went south, which to me seemed to be exactly what was happening.

While Dominic was gone, I stayed in touch with his family in Winnipeg, planning for Christmas and buying them all gifts. Despite my suspicions about Dominic, I kept acting like everything was normal. I tried to be a good wife, in case all my fears turned out to be false. I maintained the house, did all the shopping, and made everything perfect for when he came home. When he finally did return, I picked him up at the airport and gave him a big hug, but he was immediately distant. He was wearing his wedding ring, but he was very cold to me. We picked up his daughter and when we got home all his focus went to her. I felt so empty, unwanted, and in a very lonely place after having no one by my side for these last few months. I was convinced something, or rather someone, had happened to Dominic when he was in Doha, but I had no proof. Dominic was very close-lipped. I tried to get him to talk about what went on over there, but all he would say was that they were working around the clock to ensure the opening and closing ceremonies went well. I tried to remain calm and take him at his word. I wanted to trust him, even though my gut was telling me otherwise.

As we sat around the living room, I showed him the presents I bought his family, all beautifully wrapped for us to take to Winnipeg for Christmas. He went silent. Then he dropped a bomb. "I didn't buy you a plane ticket. I'm going alone with my daughter."

My heart stopped. What did I do to deserve to be left alone on Christmas? I was heartbroken. On Christmas Eve I packed up and I took my chihuahua, Duke (we got him after the Vancouver Olympics and I still have him, he was my first baby), packed up the car, and drove in tears the entire six hours to my mom and Rick's place. Dominic cried as I was leaving. Maybe it was easy not to buy me a plane ticket when he was far away in Doha, but when he was forced to see me in front of him packing the car on Christmas Eve in tears, the weight of his actions thawed his heart a little. In that moment he realized what he did wasn't right, but it was too late. I was not about to console him. Dominic and his daughter carried on to Winnipeg with the presents for his family, which he gave to them and took all the credit for.

I spent Christmas with my family trying to put on a happy face, but I was embarrassed, in shock, and really didn't know what to think. I had seen a lawyer, but deep down I hoped Dominic would come around and be my knight in shining armour, get the babysitter, and love me and we'd live happily ever after. The thought of divorce was hard to stomach at this point — not really the Christian thing to do. Part of me also didn't want to follow in my mother's footsteps with divorces and multiple marriages. I wanted to be different. And because of these deep-seated feelings, I stuck with the marriage.

Looking back on this period, I have to concede that it also had to do with my father issues. Dominic was older, and being constantly rejected by him and trying so hard to get his attention mirrored my relationship with my father. Those feelings of insecurity and vulnerability were part of my emotional DNA, and despite knowing that I deserved more, and wanted more, I kept pushing through, hoping, praying, for Dominic to want me. Getting my husband's approval was akin to getting my father's. Grown-up me can see this clearly, but in my mid-twenties I was still too young to process it. Time and distance allow for personal growth and reflection, but in that hot minute, I didn't understand what was happening. As it turned out, I wasn't the only one in my family who was having marital issues.

By this point Mom and Rick could not afford the two-bedroom condo on Palace Pier, so to help them out, I had bought a one-bedroom condo in the same building that they rented from me. However, Rick wasn't there for reasons I'll explain later. I stayed with my mom throughout the holidays all the way to New Year's

Day. In some weird way, we had fun. As usual we made the best of a tumultuous time when we both found ourselves alone without our partners during the holidays. Mom and Rick's marriage was falling apart due to his heavy drinking and lack of work and stability. Finally, my mom's trust in him was starting to waver after many of us tried to help her see the truth that he was a fraud. My brother Mike, who had also been married around the same time as me, was also going through some extreme lows. For some reason, 2012 turned out to be a very difficult year for all three of us.

After New Year's I drove back to Montreal. I didn't greet Dominic with open arms, and he didn't embrace me either. We sat down and I asked straight up if he was having an affair. He denied it. Over and over, he denied it. Finally, he said, "I just can't go on and think we should separate." I asked him if he meant divorce and he said yes. I stood up immediately and said, "No problem. I suggest you have your lawyer call mine." Then I handed him the contact information. The look on his face was priceless. He didn't expect that. I wasn't the helpless little blond housewife at home twiddling her thumbs waiting for her husband to come home. I did my due diligence. Now I needed to prove he was cheating. If I could prove that, the lawyer could file the paperwork using adultery as the cause and I could be divorced in a few months and get back financially what I put in, which was a lot of money for me at the time. If I couldn't prove an affair, then my divorce would be on the grounds of "irreconcilable differences" and could take up to two years. I wasn't about to wait, especially when I knew the truth was out there.

Over the next few weeks, we lived in the house but in separate spaces. He slept in the basement, and I remained in the upstairs room across from his daughter. We acted normal around her, and I could tell it killed him when I spent time with her and showed her gymnastics moves. He knew there would be a time when he would need to explain why, yet again, another woman had left his life.

The hard evidence of Dominic's cheating came down to old-fashioned sleuthing and technology. Skype, which was the big mode for long-distance communication in 2012, proved to be his downfall. And as I wrote at the start of this chapter, I knew his password, so I logged in and uncovered the truth. That was the night I found the messages between him and Meredith and sent them to my lawyer. After she responded that she had the evidence required for my quick divorce, I took a sip of my wine and contemplated how to express my rage. I felt as though I was in the movies, like this wasn't really my life. I took one last look at Dominic — he was such a coward — then I stood up and threw my wine glass across the living room; it smashed and splashed on the floor and made a horrific noise. His poor daughter was startled (something I regret but, in such moments, we don't always think straight) and I asked her to go to her room.

When she'd left I confronted Dominic, but he denied cheating. I asked again and again, and he denied again and again. Then I mentioned her name, Meredith. He still denied it. I mentioned parts of their conversations on Skype, and he started to panic; he was backed into a corner. But being a coward, he continued to deny, deny, deny. I told him I wasn't stupid and my lawyer had all the proof, and he would be receiving the divorce papers for adultery soon. He then broke down crying and admitted it all.

From that moment forward, I was smiling and acting happy. He had his tail between his legs like a scolded puppy. I moved back to my mom's and made Dominic pack up most of my belongings. I let him decide what to do with our framed photos and wedding albums.

I returned to the Montreal house one last time on Valentine's Day in 2012 with my mom and brother. Fitting company, as they were both going through their own relationship woes. They helped me pack up the U-Haul and I went through my mail. I found a Valentine's Day card from Meredith to Dominic. How perfect, on the one day I'm in Montreal, there's a little love note. Out of spite, and admittedly not overly mature of me, I wanted to leave a sort of *fuck you* as I moved out. I opened the card and read her endearing words, "Even though we can't be together on this Valentine's Day, we will soon be spending many more together, I love you," or something equally saccharine. I left it wide open standing upright on our kitchen counter for him to read when he got home so he'd know I had read it.

Dominic met us at a gas station, or some sort of unglamorous meet-up, to sign the divorce papers. Then I drove off in the U-Haul back to Toronto. Our relationship lasted six and a half years, with two of those years spent as a married couple. I was now twenty-six.

Despite pasting on the happy face in front of Dominic, I spent the next few weeks curled up in a ball on my mom's couch watching Adele's *Live at the Royal Albert Hall*, crying and crying. While I was recovering, having Mom wait on me hand and foot as I sat motionless on the couch was the balm I needed. She brought me presents every day to cheer me up, but soon the situation was completely reversed when she went through her own traumatic divorce.

The previous summer, my mother had had knee replacement surgery before Dominic left for Doha. When she was set to be discharged from the hospital, Rick was nowhere to be found. He was late to pick her up and wasn't answering his phone. My mom knew in her gut that something was wrong. But because she was on so many drugs and painkillers for her new knee, she didn't have the energy to question where he was at the time. Until he showed up smelling like he hadn't showered in days and reeking of booze and smoke. My mom's spirits just sank at the sight of him. They made it back to the condo, and as my mom entered, in immense pain, they saw that the place had been ransacked. It was like a crime scene. Whoever had broken in had searched the place and taken anything of value.

Rick was completely shocked. How could a break-in happen in a building with a concierge and security? My mother had left all her jewellery at home because she couldn't have it at the hospital. Granted, she didn't own many expensive items; they were mainly sentimental pieces. She was in immense pain and went straight to bed, overwhelmed and needing to sleep. Over the course of the next few days, she asked more questions about the incident, all of which Rick brushed off. She looked for her missing jewellery to no avail. Cabinets had been opened, but nothing else really seemed to be missing. Especially none of Rick's belongings. But my mother noticed there was also money missing from their bank account. Money was tight, so every penny counted for them. He pretended not to know anything about it. My mother was still recovering and didn't push him.

By the time I arrived for Christmas in 2011 after the Dominic and plane ticket debacle, Rick was already staying at a hotel part-time. Mom and Rick underwent Christian counselling after the robbery because, like her children, she knew something major had happened, between his being late to pick her up, showing up drunk, and this crazy robbery story that no one believed. My mom said she wanted separate bank accounts, and it was this decision that ultimately made him pack up (with a push from me) because he could see she was serious about uncovering the truth and not believing his lies anymore.

Fast forward to late January when I'd moved back in with her, an email arrived from Rick documenting every detail of what transpired that night. Call it Christian guilt on his part for coming clean. But the email made my mom put her head in her hands in dismay, complete and utter shock and disgust. The night in question, when Mom was in the hospital, Rick was at a strip joint, and he picked up a stripper or a prostitute and brought her back to the condo. They smoked crack cocaine together and she proceeded to steal all of my mother's jewellery. Then she convinced Rick they needed more drugs and to drive her from Etobicoke to Scarborough to get them. But first they stopped at an ATM and withdrew hundreds of dollars from his and my mother's joint account. Rick proceeded to give the lady the money, and she told him to wait in the car while she went to get more drugs. She never came back. Then he overslept the next day, remembered what had transpired, and staged a break-in as a cover-up. Then he arrived late to pick up my mother at the hospital. This was supposed to be a man of God. I know the Bible says, "Do not judge, or you too will be judged. For in the same way you judge others, you will be judged, and with the measure you use, it will be measured to you" (Matthew 7:1–2). But in this instance, I couldn't help but judge how any human could do this to another person, let alone someone I love.

The moment I found out the whole truth, I grabbed all of his belongings that remained in the condo and took them down to the underground parking in the elevator and piled them on top of his car. Not inside, on top and around for everyone to see that he was kicked out. I proceeded to the security and concierge desk and removed his name from accessing the building. Since I owned the unit, I had that authority. I informed security that when Rick arrived from whatever job he had at the time, they were to direct him to the basement to collect his belongings and get the hell out. I was quite proud of that. And that was the end of Rick.

Today, whenever Rick comes up, or Stan, or even my father for that matter, my mother is very calm and matter-of-fact, she's made peace with the past. The reason is her faith. She has forgiven them. When I ask her why she's not bitter or how she can forgive such transgressions, her answer is simple, and as you'd expect, from the Bible: "If I want to be forgiven, I have to forgive others." And being my mother's daughter, I would eventually forgive Dominic, but I wasn't there yet.

If things weren't bad enough for Mom and me, as I mentioned, my brother Mike was going through a divorce at the same time. His wife had also cheated on him in January of that year during a girls' trip down south. He found out in the worst of ways by finding some photos on social media. A few months after their marriage imploded, Mike and I were at the liquor store, shopping for whatever party we were throwing, since our breakups had been finalized, and we ran into the man his wife had cheated on him with. While we were shopping, I saw Mike's face go white, maybe even green, like he was about to throw up. I looked across the aisle and there he was, "the other man."

I whispered to Mike to "wait here," and I marched off. He tried to stop me, but I was on a mission. I stepped in front of the man who was sleeping with Mike's then-wife, and I started to flirt with him. I kept smiling and repeating, "I know you from somewhere, I know you from somewhere."

He seemed pleased that I was giving him my time and attention, until I said very loudly, "Oh that's right, you're the man who's fucking my brother's wife."

The entire store turned toward him in disgust and couldn't believe I had just made a scene like one from a rom-com. Then I marched back to Mike, who by now was smirking but also shocked, and I said simply, "Okay, what else do we need for the party?"

I don't know where the guts or confidence came from at that moment, but I was so tired of cheaters who thought they could get away with their actions without consequences. Needless to say, the first half of 2012, with myself, my mother, and my brother going through divorces simultaneously, was very difficult, but at the same time we leaned on each other and got through it. Blood is thicker than water, and thicker than bad marriages, too.

Sometime during that winter, Dominic called me in tears, apologizing for everything, begging me to come back and forgive him. It was too late. Meredith was literally on her way from Australia and had left her husband for Dominic. I was so tempted to tell her he had called asking for me back, but he was her problem now. I got many emails from Dominic's family asking what had happened and I didn't hesitate to tell them every detail. They were in shock. Though after our conversations, I felt as though they knew Dominic had a problem with relationships, and they told me he just didn't seem to be able to commit to anyone.

And to put a final punctuation mark on this chapter in my life, a male friend of Dominic's family reached out to me in 2014. He had supported my side of things throughout the marital breakdown, and we'd kept in touch. He was more than twice my age, and he met me for dinner once in Toronto while he was in town on business. I always felt he had my back, and I could confide in him because he was such a close family friend. I paid for dinner to thank him for being so kind during my divorce. He wanted to treat me to a drink at the bar as a thank-you for buying him dinner, but he said he needed to grab his wallet (or a gift he forgot, I can't remember) in his hotel room. Thinking nothing of it, since he was a gracious man, I went with him. Before I knew it, he opened his hotel room door and leaned in to do I'm not sure what, but it was some sort of clumsy sexual advance, and when I backed away, he grabbed me and tried to pull me into his room. I escaped his grasp and ran down the hall and pressed the elevator button over and over until it came. Then, once I was in the lobby, I ran outside and jumped into a taxi. I called Mike on the way home crying. He wanted to go over there and confront him, but I said to leave it, we needed to move on from that family. What a mess.

Dominic called again a few years later, checking to see how I was doing and to let me know he and Meredith had broken up. I wasn't surprised because his daughter often texted me and told me how much she disliked Meredith and that she missed me. Funny how Dominic thought our relationship wasn't strong, yet after I was long gone, she still confided in me. Dominic said he grew to hate Meredith, but felt he was punishing himself by staying with her as a form of redemption. He couldn't believe he blew up our marriage to be with her.

I did as my mother had, I told him I forgave him and ended the call amicably. I felt at peace, and I think he was able to move on from that point forward as well. Once again, my mother's influence and my own faith had brought me through a tumultuous period and made me stronger.

During all this personal turmoil, I reconnected with old friends from my gymnastics days. They were women who also lived in Toronto, many of them single, and I became somewhat of a party girl about town. It was as though I was making up for all those high school years in my mid-twenties. I also looked for a so-called normal job. I tried public relations, which made sense to me, since I had my degree in the field. But the entry-level salaries were so far below what I'd earned as a performer that I turned them down. I wound up working at a boring desk job to make ends meet, but I lived for 5 p.m. and the weekends when I was free to hang out with my friends. I didn't date anyone seriously or special either, I was over men and commitment, at least for now. But I also felt lost, adrift in this new life that didn't quite feel fully mine yet. Then the opportunity I'd been waiting for arrived in the form of USA Gymnastics Federation asking me to be one of the creative directors for its 2012 post–London Olympics gymnastics tour. This was the exact same concept as I had done in 2004 as an athlete. Only this time around, because of my experience at Cirque du Soleil, the organization had enough faith in me to ask me to choreograph, direct, and perform in the tour. My sixth life was about to officially begin!

The tour showcased the Olympic women's gold medal–winning team, as well as individual all-around champion Gabby Douglas. Big names like Aly Raisman, Jordyn Wieber, and McKayla Maroney were also on the tour and helped sell out our shows every night. Nastia Liukin, who won the all-around gold in 2008, also joined the show and shined doing aerial tricks no one had ever seen her do before. I had her visit me in Toronto prior to the tour to help get her ready and train her in aerial skills. She was a natural. Chellsie Memmel also joined the tour and made history because, after retirement, getting married, and having two kids, she made a comeback to the sport. The men were also incredible and performed to tracks like LMFAO's "Sexy and I Know It." They had charisma galore, and were definitely sexy enough that more than one female audience member could be seen blushing from their overt display of masculinity.

The creation of the show was tough, since coming off the Olympics, the gymnasts were tired and injured, so keeping a certain level of gymnastics was always a struggle, but we persevered and got standing ovations every night. It was gruelling. You trained, did rehearsals, performed at night, got on the tour bus, slept for a few hours, checked in to hotels at two or three in the morning, tried to go back to sleep, and woke up and did it all over again. Living the rockstar life was fun and exciting, but always exhausting. Especially because I wasn't only performing, I also had to watch the show, take notes, and make sure the next show was even better than the last. Constantly evolving and improving the show was tiring, but we didn't have much time to put it together, so it was necessary to make the changes throughout. It was my favourite show to date. Partially because I created every aspect of it with my co-creative director, John Macready, a 1996 Olympian, so we felt like our hearts were in it completely.

Also on tour were the usual physiotherapists and doctors. The athletes suffered from various injuries following the Olympics, and they needed as much support as possible before and after each show. I was also injured. I had retired from competitive sport in 2004. However, Cirque du Soleil and the ten shows per week really did a number on my body. I was broken. My ankles, toes, back, ribs, and hips were a mess, and I needed constant physiotherapy. I also wasn't training as much as I should have because I was too busy managing and choreographing. So I basically went out every night and performed cold with little rehearsal, which was the worst thing you could possibly do to your body. Especially when you were performing aerial acts. I often got too loose, so my joints shifted all around because I wasn't strengthening or doing enough conditioning.

One of the doctors that visited the tour was the now-convicted rapist Larry Nassar, but in 2012 he was still the USA Gymnastics head doctor and had been working with the governing body for more than twenty years. It's tough to imagine that only three years later the truth of what he had done would explode into an international scandal that would bring shame and horror to the sport. An astounding 265 young women and girls alleged that he had repeatedly sexually assaulted them, using his "medical treatments" to cover up the assaults. In 2017 he was sentenced to sixty years in federal prison after pleading guilty to child pornography and tampering with evidence. Then in 2018 he was sentenced to an additional forty years after pleading guilty to seven counts of sexual assault of minors.

I had seen him throughout my career for my turf toe without incident. But during this latest tour, I had thrown a rib out of place. This was a common injury for me. I was doing my specialty act of contortion and hanging on a small jumping-rope apparatus, and sometimes the rope slid between my ribs and caused them to shift. It was painful and made it difficult to breathe. Larry happened to be on the tour when I got hurt, so I asked him if he could take a look at my rib. The therapy room was bursting with activity. Other gymnasts from the show were being treated by the various medical staff. Larry directed me to his area, and I laid on the table on my back. I explained where the pain was and that it had happened before at Cirque and that likely my rib was out of place. I had gotten used to the pain, but it was excruciating. Larry immediately knew what to do. He shifted me on my left side to face the wall, he placed his hand up my shirt and started to feel around, and immediately found which rib was out. He quickly adjusted me, stretched me, and had me take some deep breaths to test if I could breathe normally. I was instantly better. But he wasn't done with me. Larry continued to massage my ribs, then he placed a hand inside my sports bra, so his bare hand was on my breast. I thought to myself, *This is weird*, but I guessed it was my upper left rib that was out, so he needed to massage around the area to ensure it would stay in place. Or at least that's what I told myself. He continued to rub my breast and the area around it, then I felt him pinching my nipple. I was in shock. Why, in a room full of people, were his hands up my bra? As I was thinking this, too stunned to react, he began rubbing both my breasts and squeezing them with his hand, as his other hand pressed against my back so I couldn't move. I then realized I was facing the wall, and no one could see what he was doing. It all happened so quickly. He then removed his hand, adjusted my bra, and placed me on my back. He continued to check my alignment and talk throughout the entire incident, which was even more confusing. How he was able to hold a conversation while adjusting my rib, molesting me, and fixing my alignment is some real multitasking. He asked how my breathing was, sat me up, and showed me some exercises to enable me to prevent my rib from moving out of place again, and I was on my way. I thanked him (that's how shocked I was) and walked out of the physio room in a daze, but quickly noticed that my pain was gone, and that was the top priority. I quickly dismissed what had happened, thinking it must have just been me overthinking things, and carried on with my day. I went to training, modified some of the tour routines with the gymnasts, had dinner, and did my hair and makeup for the show.

One of the staff members walked into the dressing room where I was getting ready, and we were talking about the changes we were to implement that night. I mentioned to him, "You know, the craziest thing happened to me at physio today. I'm pretty sure Larry just molested me. His hands were all up my bra after he had fixed my rib, having a field day." The staff member just laughed and said, "You're crazy, there's no way Larry would ever do that." I shrugged it off and laughed to myself and went on to do the show. I never thought about that moment or told anyone until many years down the road. Yet obviously, it bothered me enough to mention it.

The tour was the most successful of its kind in USA Gymnastics history. We sold out almost every arena and the profits were through the roof. The gymnasts were incredible and gave it their all. I was so honoured, and so proud of each one of them. I loved creating that show and performing alongside them. It taught me that creating and performing was what I loved to do.

I returned to Toronto and got another boring desk job to pay the bills while I tried to figure out what was next. I couldn't stand it, the entertainment bug had bitten again, I knew that was where my future lay, but exactly how it would manifest was the mystery. As the years went by, I had lots of fun on evenings and weekends with my friends, mostly former gymnasts but other women, too, but my days were terrible. Sitting at a desk, doing a job I hated, I counted the hours until I could leave. I continued to do freelance gigs, which kept me spiritually alive. I was the backstage manager for a few Cirque events and continued to perform in "animation" gigs here and there for them. Animation is when you roam an audience before the big event. You are not the star or showcase; you are simply there to look pretty and distract the audience during a cocktail hour. It's not a glamorous gig, but Cirque paid very well so I kept doing them. I bought my own condo downtown on Lake Ontario and lived alone. I was so proud of that condo. It was a beautiful one-bedroom with stunning views of the city and the water. It had beautiful sunsets, and I felt at peace when I was there. It was my first real home.

But toward the end of 2014, I was lost yet again. I was only finding happiness by going out with my friends, and I'd lost sight of who I wanted to be. I was single and didn't want to settle down or date seriously. I knew I needed to figure out who I was and who I wanted to be before I could truly make anyone else happy. Then thankfully, USA Gymnastics returned with another tantalizing offer: They wanted me to be their creative director for the 2016 post–Rio de Janeiro Olympics gymnastics tour. I needed this. But it was still years away. I had to find happiness and fulfillment now, which meant a new career path. I like to think that my sixth life wasn't over, it just needed a companion, a seventh life I could do at the same time, and yet another reinvention.

## What I Learned

**Reason:** During this phase of my life, my reasons to get out of bed and thrive vacillated between being a good wife and partner and a special events performer. But they weren't enough; my marriage and the Cirque gigs no longer made me want to jump out of bed with enthusiasm. I was lucky then, when I was given the opportunity to fulfill my goal of creative director for the gymnastics tour. It gave me the reason I needed.

**Reinvent:** I had to reinvent myself twice, first after my marriage fell apart, and then when I threw myself into that gymnastics tour. I was a newly minted choreographer and creative director.

**Right:** This one is easy to say, but hard to do. I had the right to leave my unhappy marriage. It took a lot of strength, and for one of the first times in my life, admit failure. We all have the right to fail and move on. We have the right to leave a relationship where we aren't happy and aren't thriving. We have the right to happiness.

O

Lives Five and Six, soloist and choreographer/creative director respectively, were put on hold for now. Next up, Life Seven ...

# 7<sup>TH</sup> LIFE:

# ENTERTAINMENT EXECUTIVE

I'm in a Los Angeles studio watching my new boss, Robert Herjavec, and his partner, Kym Johnson, rehearse for a segment on *Dancing with the Stars*. I love choreography and find the creation of the dances more inspiring than the live performances. My time is spent getting smoothies, Band-Aids, whatever Robert and Kym need leading up to the show each Monday. But this week is different, it's more emotional for Robert, and deep down, for me. But I keep my feelings to myself, holding back tears, as I watch the duo practise a waltz in honour of Robert's mother. The theme for the next episode is "most memorable year." Robert's most memorable year was when he lost his mother. She was his biggest fan and had once told him she hoped he'd appear on *Dancing with the Stars* because she was a huge fan of the show and watched it faithfully each week with her friends. She passed away from ovarian cancer in 2006. Robert is visibly emotional during the practice. This waltz means everything.

As I stand watching Robert and Kym, my mind drifts to my most memorable year, the 2004 Athens Olympics and everything it took to get me there. Robert's story is similar to mine, and makes me think about my father, who was my biggest fan and believed in me, his "little Olympian," before he died from cancer when I was eight. It also brings to mind my mother's sacrifices, and I know she, too, would love to see me on *Dancing with the Stars*, expressing my many lives to the world through dance. And in that moment, a future dream crystalizes: To be on the show and get the chance that Robert didn't have, to dance with my mother for my most memorable year. I see it so vividly, my mom and I dancing away all the hardships to Adele's "Hello," a song with so much meaning to us. I hope one day I can make this dream come true.

○

I knew I needed to discover a new passion, one that would allow me the freedom to continue working as a performer and choreographer, yet be fulfilling to me while I paid the bills. And as has occurred time and again in my life, it came about unexpectedly. Here's what happened.

It was late fall 2014, and as I said, I felt lost and hated the desk job I had at the time. So I began searching for another position and came across a posting that was one of the vaguest I'd ever seen. I had no idea who or what the Herjavec Group was, and the posting was literally a paragraph with not much information other than that it was an executive assistant position supporting the CEO of a company. I had a lot of experience with C-level executives at Cirque du Soleil, USA Gymnastics, and the United States Olympic Committee. And being an executive assistant was a people game, and I'm good at reading people.

Before applying I did my research and learned the Herjavec Group was a cybersecurity company, and the CEO, Robert

Herjavec, was a "shark" on the reality series *Shark Tank* and had previously been on *Dragons' Den*. I didn't watch either show, and really had no interest whatsoever in cybersecurity, but thought, why not apply and see what happens? As you know by now, I'm a big believer in God having a plan if it's meant to be.

Almost immediately, I got an email requesting a phone interview from his current executive assistant, a lovely woman named Emily. It turned out that the job was a one-year maternity leave contract, not a full-time position, which I thought was perfect because I would do this contract and be done just in time for my 2016 Olympic tour. I had the phone interview and immediately admired and connected with Emily. She was organized, confident, and knew Robert inside and out. I felt hers were big shoes to fill, but I was always up for a challenge. I still didn't know much about Robert, but I think that may have helped me in the end. Everything good in my life to this point had happened when I least expected it, so why should this be any different?

I went on to have about four rounds of interviews before meeting Robert. He was travelling a lot, so I had gone into the offices on numerous occasions to meet other members of the team. I met co-founders, chief information officers, heads of marketing and sales, chief business officers, you name it. I felt like I had met the entire company yet not the person I would be reporting to and supporting day to day. It was an intense process, but I knew selecting an executive assistant was a big deal for a company. You are the gatekeeper for all things personal and professional for that CEO. I wasn't surprised at the numerous steps and hoops to jump through, but I was anxious to see if Robert and I connected.

At last, when we finally met, we did connect. He was energetic, down-to-earth, and had a confidence about him that was contagious. I immediately felt we could work well together. Apparently, he felt the same because shortly after our meeting I was offered the position and was given a start date of January 5, 2015. It was around Christmas time when I got the news, so it was nice to resign from the desk job I despised and enjoy the holidays knowing that I was going to be starting the new year with an exciting opportunity. Granted, I really didn't know what was ahead in the role, but I knew I would be learning a lot and it would look good on my resumé.

I arrived early on my first day because I was always taught that being on time is being late. I had my orientation, and I sat with Emily to learn the ropes. I was the new girl in town, so of course I felt a lot of eyes on me, nothing I wasn't used to from being on stage. I knew the first few weeks would be very telling, so I put my best foot forward and tried to grasp and absorb as much as I could.

Robert wasn't around much during my few weeks of training. Then one day, while I was sitting at Emily's desk, she told me that Robert wanted me in Los Angeles because he had decided to move there full-time and needed an extra set of hands. The reason for the abrupt change of locale was that Robert had been asked to be a celebrity on *Dancing with the Stars*, which I thought that was the coolest thing, and of course I agreed to pack up and head south. I had been to Los Angeles before but only passing through for work, so I was game for more adventures.

I arrived in Los Angeles not knowing exactly what was required of me. I knew I needed to keep up with my corporate responsibilities, but in terms of the personal side of things, I didn't know what he expected from me. It turned out that Robert had purchased a house and needed help setting it up so he could work from there while filming *Dancing with the Stars*. It was a fun project and I quickly started navigating around Los Angeles and learning the best shops for decor, food, and everything in between. As it turned out, Emilie, a former teammate from my childhood, also lived in Los Angeles, so she showed me all the hot spots and made me feel like a piece of home was there with me.

During this time, I worked from my hotel room, dashing out to run errands for Robert when required. Sitting at a desk day in and day out wasn't for me, so I really liked constantly being on the move. I swiftly became comfortable in my new role and soon didn't need much guidance from Emily back in Toronto. Robert's life was different now. He lived in a different country, and I was by his side day in and day out to help him get to where he needed to be, so I took my direction from him. I think people back at the Toronto office wondered how I got up to speed so quickly. It wasn't really a mystery; I dedicated my days and evenings to Robert and enjoyed every moment of it. When you love your job, you give it your all and it becomes a part of you. Learning the ropes becomes natural and you begin to excel without even trying. Being surrounded by the Hollywood life was also exciting. I loved the feeling that at any moment your life could change forever because you never knew who you might meet.

Shortly after I arrived, Robert began rehearsing with his dance partner (and now wife), Kym Johnson. Kym is lovely and a very patient and kind person. She was as down-to-earth as Robert, and I think taught him a lot about appreciating the simple things in life. Robert was always so head-down-in-business that I think meeting Kym was a breath of fresh air. She taught him not only how to dance, but also to love to dance and perform. Dance has a way of speaking to people. Whether you are dancing for yourself or to please others, it's a powerful form of art. It can be emotional, uplifting, or heartbreaking. I loved dancing in my gymnastics and stage career, so I was happy to see Robert find himself through dance as well, and was honoured to witness it first-hand.

As fate would have it, I knew some of the other celebrities who appeared during Robert's season of *Dancing with the Stars*. Redfoo was one of them; he had previously been a guest performer on my 2012 gymnastics tour. We'd flown together during my aerial act while he sang "Party Rock Anthem." He was so full of life and was a real character, and he always dressed in the flashiest of clothes. We'd had an entire floor routine devoted to his hits on our tour, so it was fun to see him during the production of *Dancing with the Stars*. Then there was Nastia Liukin, who was also on the 2012 gymnastics tour. For *Dancing with the Stars* she was partnered with the incredible Derek Hough. Of course, she shined every night and was a complete showstopper. Her long lines and elegant demeanor made the crowd speechless. To be honest, I thought she would win the season. It was incredible to see all my worlds colliding in this strangest of circumstances, and on a Hollywood soundstage, no less! Robert was also amazed that I knew so much of the cast. He kept asking me, "Who are you?" because I seemed to know everyone. There were also production crew members that I knew from my Cirque days. The entertainment space is a small world. Up until that moment, I don't think Robert really grasped my previous life, and he no doubt wondered how I came to be so connected. But I had been touring the world and working as an entertainer for close to ten years, so I fit right in on the set.

Another aspect of the job that I loved was attending the live shows each week. One reason was that I loved dressing up. I also hosted mini-celebrations in Robert's trailer after each show for him, Kym, and any of his guests who had flown in to watch the action. It was fascinating to observe these people. They came to the show, but they knew Robert as a business icon, and were not used to seeing him in this more emotional, creative light. He was a serious businessman, a shark on *Shark Tank*, yet here he was performing with his shirt unbuttoned and dancing with passion. He gave it his all and the whole world saw that. All who came to see him were mesmerized. We often went to dinner afterward, and his friends and colleagues were always in awe of his performance.

My hat was off to Kym because she was able to take Robert and transform him into a dancer in so little time. That is not an easy task at all. There were many celebrities that came and went on the show and didn't improve or adapt to choreography. Robert wasn't one of them. He was able to understand the vision for each week's performance. As I wrote in the opening of this chapter, he dedicated the waltz to his mother, and it brought the entire house to tears. That is talent. That right there shows you that you don't have to be a professional dancer to touch someone's heart. If you perform with intent and purpose, you can convey your story and let people feel your purpose. Robert was performing with his heart and meant every step he took on the floor with all his being. He and Kym made a good team. Eventually, they started to make a good team off the dance floor. I was there the day they met, and I've been by their side throughout their love story. It's been a remarkable experience and I'm very blessed to know the two of them. And now I know their twins, Hudson and Haven, who are a reflection of their love.

As the season was nearing its end, we were all getting tired. I attended rehearsals and ran errands for Robert during the day and worked on my corporate responsibilities at night. I had been in Los Angeles a few months and was starting to hit a wall. But I kept pushing through because I loved my job. Every week I continued to arrange travel, meetings, after-show dinners, and ground transportation. It was a 24/7 job. Ultimately, Robert didn't win the mirror ball trophy, but he was very pleased with his experience on the show.

After *Dancing with the Stars* wrapped, Robert began filming the next season of *Shark Tank* at Sony Studios, also in Los Angeles. I got to meet all the sharks, including Mark Cuban, Daymond John, Kevin O'Leary, Barbara Corcoran, and Lori Greiner. I began to work on set alongside their teams as they closed deals and partnered. I learned a lot about the due diligence involved with investing and acquisitions. I also liked the variety of deals that the sharks did. Sometimes it involved investing in a clothing line or cleaning product, and other times it was a food product or some sort of gaming device. All of it was confidential, so you couldn't take photos because the episodes wouldn't air until months later. However, I did manage to snag a few photos of myself in the shark's hot seat.

On one occasion Robert flew my brother Matt out to the set for his birthday, which was incredibly kind of him. I missed my family, and Matt was quite the entrepreneur, so I knew he would love visiting the set. Matt was there every day to watch filming, and he couldn't keep his eyes off the pitches. He was so invested and was the first person there in the morning and the last one to leave at night. I came and went, and when I returned, he was still sitting in the same spot as when I had left. I admired his passion for the show and the businesses. He later moved to Rome, Italy, and became a CEO in his own business ventures.

It was wonderful to be behind the scenes on *Shark Tank*, but eventually even that got old for me. The pitches were sometimes close to two hours in length, a far cry from the five- to ten-minute segments they aired on TV. Eventually, I stopped spending the entire day in the studio and returned to my hotel to get my corporate work done so I could have some downtime in the evenings.

As *Shark Tank* filming wrapped in the fall, I continued to live out of a suitcase. The job was so all-encompassing that I didn't have much time for myself. I was homesick and began to fly back and forth from Los Angeles to Toronto almost weekly, but it wasn't easy with the time change and length of the flight. I got ill a few times. I wasn't eating properly and spent too much time in airports or on planes. I was devoting my life to my job and letting myself get run down. Also, for the few days I was back home, I reunited with my friends and stayed out late and was exhausted the next day, but didn't let anything drop at work. It wasn't sustainable.

Eventually, Robert had to spend more time in Toronto for his business, so I made the full move back. At this point it was late in

2015 and I had spent an entire year on the road. I was exhausted but happy to be back in Toronto in the condo I was so proud of. I started to work from the Toronto head office again. I was doing well in my job and had my own office next to Robert's in the executive wing. I was living full-time in the corporate world. It was a massive shift and a culture shock. It wasn't as exciting as my time in Los Angeles, and I wasn't sure if I would like it. That's why, without even realizing it at the time, I was evolving into my seventh life: Entertainment executive. Little did I know that by 2021 I'd be named vice-president of entertainment and global partnerships for Herjavec Entertainment Corp., creating partnerships, endorsements with global brands, and along with a team, developing original content for networks and live events. But first, there would be another national gymnastics tour to bring to life, and a health crisis to overcome.

As the year came to an end, the 2016 gymnastics tour that I'd signed up to create was set to start up after the Olympics in Rio de Janeiro. I only had a few months left on my contract with Robert, so I started to develop and conceptualize the tour in my spare time. I listened to music and choreographed in my living room into the wee hours of the night. I always came alive at night. That was my routine on the road with Cirque. After a year in a corporate role, I felt my body come alive again as I developed the 2016 tour. Working both gigs was a good balance, and I was focused and excited about all the visions and concepts that were coming to me. The 2012 tour had been a test for me to see if I could create a two-hour live touring show and if it could be successful. With the success of that tour under my belt, I was going into creating the 2016 tour with a whole new level of confidence.

I was still going to perform, but only in an aerial act. I had designed an aerial bubble number and would perform in straps and hammocks (which are like circus silks in a U shape). I was a bit out of shape, given the commitment to my job with Robert. My strength was not at its best, especially for aerial work. I began working out but not exactly doing professional circus aerial training. You can work out all you want, but every aerial acrobat will tell you that unless you are regularly flying in the air supporting your own body weight and doing your skills, nothing can prepare you for it, not even if you go to the gym three times a day. An aerialist must support and contort their body into all kinds of positions, while mentally staying focused, because death is only twenty or more feet below. As the tour approached, I grew anxious because I hadn't had time to prepare for the aerial requirements, but I felt I could make it work — I had to. My creative partner from the last tour, John Macready, and I had stepped it up a level. This was going to be the best tour in USA Gymnastics history and surpass the success we had in 2012.

While I was in Toronto creating the show, still working at Herjavec Group, and juggling the busiest year of my career, I met a man who would turn out to be my second husband and the love of my life. It's funny how when you have your head down and you're not looking for it, you meet a person who will change your life forever. Yet when you're looking and longing for that person, they are nowhere to be found. I believe that my husband and I needed to find one another when we did. He immediately completed me. He was my rock and had my whole heart from the beginning. He changed me for the better. It terrified me, but for some reason I knew I could trust him. And trust wasn't something I did easily due to my past. He understood me, accepted my past, and promised me that I would never have to worry again. I felt safe.

It's a funny story about how David and I met. One night, I was with one of my best friends, we were having a night of wine and food and girl talk. She had mentioned how there were all these dating apps and I should try one. I had heard of them but didn't think I would find anyone worth my time that way. I also had no interest in dating. A couple glasses of wine later and I agreed to let my friend install Tinder on my phone. We started swiping left and right. I had no idea what she was doing so I grabbed my phone to have a look. I stumbled across David's profile and swiped right. We matched and started talking right away. We exchanged social handles and his first question to me was "You look normal and successful, what's wrong with you?" Anyone who knows my husband knows that this is his personality. Straight to the point and no bullshit. I went on to tell him I'd been burned in the past, was a workaholic, travelled a lot for my job, and wasn't looking for anything serious. He felt the same and so we soon met up, and the rest is history. I will be forever grateful to my friend for convincing me to download Tinder and meet my husband that night. It was like we'd been searching for each other all our lives.

However, I couldn't have met him at a worse time, because I was very dedicated to both my day job and my job as creative director for the tour. David worked a lot as well. He managed an entire food plant with multiple offices across North America, so his hands were very full. We bonded over the fact that we didn't come from a lot of money and had to work hard for what we had. I could never be with someone who had a sense of entitlement or had a spoiled bone in their body. I always believed that you need to work hard for your success. Nothing in life is owed, deserved, or handed to you, and if you're lucky enough to achieve some success with no effort, it doesn't teach you anything or help you in future situations. Robert always said, "The only thing the world owes you is opportunity." It's true and I stand by that quote.

David and I were on the same page from the start, and he supported my busy schedule and high career aspirations. He had been a single guy in Toronto for a while and was ready to settle down, get married, and have a family. I wasn't quite there yet — I needed to accomplish a few dreams and goals of mine before I could even think of having kids. My body was still very much my profession.

It's so hard for women because our careers are often put on hold and our dreams must pause when we have kids. Granted, kids are a blessing, but I didn't like the social pressure to put your life on hold for a family. I felt you could have it all. You could get married, have kids, and continue your career. We are often penalized or experience prejudice when pregnant. I had seen it a few times with my friends who were in steady employment. Once they got pregnant, they were treated differently leading up to their maternity leave. Then, once they returned, they were treated differently, sometimes unfairly, and often got demoted and that promotion they were once lined up for had disappeared. This was probably because their boss knew that in a few years they would want another baby to grow their family. All this to say that while I was excited to meet David and was very grateful to have him by my side, I needed time before I dealt with all the pressures that come with marriage and having a family.

In a surprise turn of events, as I neared the end of my contract and the start of the tour, Emily decided not to return as Robert's executive assistant, instead she was moving to another opportunity within the company. I was offered a full-time job and I accepted. I liked the stability, but also knew I was going to be away for three months in the fall of the same year. There was no way I wouldn't do the tour, so I approached Robert and told him the situation and that for every Olympic cycle it was very important for me to do a passion project like this. I needed to always honour and do something with my gymnastics and Olympic roots because it was part of who I was. Robert understood and granted me permission to do the tour and work remotely for him. What had I gotten myself into? My job supporting Robert the person, and the Herjavec Group business, was an around-the-clock job, and the tour was also around-the-clock but on the road. It was going to be even more crazy than I'd ever imagined.

Needless to say, I found it difficult to balance my new relationship, new job, the tour commitment, and my old friends. I felt I never had enough time for everyone and often found myself trying to please everyone else. The ulcers I had at Cirque after my injury were returning, and my stomach was raw, which made me feel flu-like and weak with a dull achy feeling in the pit of my stomach. I was also tired all the time even after I had stayed in and gotten twelve hours of sleep. It was this extreme level of exhaustion that started to concern me. It was clear my health was deteriorating. I was getting sick often with strep throat or fevers. I could barely get out of bed. When I was driving back and forth to my job, my eyes were getting blurry and I was almost blacking out. I needed to change something in my life, otherwise I wasn't to survive the year ahead. I couldn't ignore the symptoms any longer. I went to see a doctor.

My mind went to worst-case scenarios immediately. I thought I had cancer like my father, or some other life-threatening disease. They ran the usual tests and I had to wait several days for the results. When the doctor's office called to ask me to come in to discuss the findings, I panicked. I was convinced this was the end. I got to the office and sat on the examination table, and the doctor asked me questions about my daily routine, what I ate, when I ate, and if I travelled a lot to foreign countries. It was bizarre. I thought, *Why is he asking me about my diet and my schedule?*

He went on to point out that my blood work revealed I was severely vitamin B12 deficient. So deficient that I was at risk for brain damage and serious side effects. I had no idea what B12 was and no idea how I had become so deficient. The doctor went on to tell me that not having enough B12 can lead to anemia, which means your body doesn't have enough red blood cells to do the job. This can make you feel weak and tired. Vitamin B12 deficiency can cause damage to your nerves and can affect memory and thinking. I'd had anemia when I was a gymnast. When I was cutting food and not eating after three in the afternoon to lose weight, I quickly developed anemia and had zero energy. This time around though, I wasn't dieting, I wasn't intentionally cutting food, I was just busy. So busy that I forgot to eat half the time, and when I did eat, it was something salty and not nutritious. I had unintentionally made myself sick and put everyone and my career before my health. I was mad at myself.

The doctor went on to explain that since our bodies don't make vitamin B12, we must get it from animal-based foods or from supplements. He also explained that I should be eating more animal-based foods on a regular basis, because our bodies don't store vitamin B12 for a long time. All of this was news to me. I had never heard of B12. I knew a lot of vegetarians that steered clear of animal-based food products, and yet I'd never heard this mentioned by any of them. How in the world did I have this deficiency and they didn't?

Inevitably, my poor eating habits had caught up to me and the doctor was worried. I had a lot of the more serious symptoms, which included fatigue, weakness, anemia, strange sensations, numbness or tingling in my hands, legs, and feet, difficulty thinking and reasoning (cognitive difficulties) or memory loss, especially at work. I couldn't hold a thought very long and had a very hard time concentrating due to my fatigue and blurred vision. The doctor was concerned that my lack of vitamin B12 was causing permanent nerve damage and potentially degeneration of the spinal cord. Lack of B12 can damage the area that surrounds and protects the nerves, and even a mild deficiency may affect the nervous system and the proper functioning of the brain. The nerve damage caused by lack of B12 may become permanently debilitating if the condition isn't treated. Vitamin B12 deficiency and the resulting increase in homocysteine levels can lead to brain atrophy.

Everything my doctor was telling me completely freaked me out. I had given myself nerve and brain damage from not paying enough attention to my health. I asked him if I needed surgery or to stop working and he laughed and said no. I needed to start taking B12 supplements daily and to eat more animal-based proteins. That was it! I was shocked. He said I would start to feel better almost right away after taking supplements, since my body had been deficient for so long, and I would see an immediate difference.

He was right. I went to the pharmacy and purchased B12 supplements and almond milk and went home and drank the whole thing. My doctor told me that while soy, almond, and rice milks are not naturally high in vitamin B12, they are usually fortified, which makes them an excellent source of B12. I felt instantly better, and I woke up the next few days like a different woman. I was so grateful to my doctor who caught this before it was too late. My health was more important and if I was a few pounds heavier, so be it. I'd rather that than brain damage!

As I got my health back on track, I continued creating the tour and doing my day job. The personal side of my executive assistant role was very busy because Robert was gearing up to get married to Kym. I had to oversee many aspects of this Hollywood wedding and it was very time-consuming and involved quite a few trips back and forth to Los Angeles. The wedding planning was stressful, no surprise there! I oversaw the entire guest list and non-disclosure agreements from all vendors and those in attendance. I also had to plan pre-events leading up to the big day, all while juggling my regular corporate job duties. It was a lot once again, and I could feel the ulcers in my stomach throughout. I was spending a lot of time away from home again, too. I missed David, my friends, and my family. Soon after the wedding, I'd be departing for three months on tour as well, so I tried to just take every day as it came and do my best. But once again, a health issue lay in wait for me.

It happened one morning in the summer of 2016 while I was in Toronto preparing to head out to Los Angeles, I woke up and couldn't move my upper body. I felt stuck, as though the lights in my upper body had been switched off. I could move my legs and toes, but I just could not move my arms. I couldn't even move my head side to side. If I tried to move anything from my waist up, I had excruciating pain like lightning bolts through my body and my neck. I had done a one-off aerial gig a week prior to see what sort of shape I was in before the tour. It had gone well, I felt heavy, but I knew I would be okay after a little more practice. I did all my usual skills, including hanging from my neck and toes. I felt great after the event, and a week had already passed and I was fine.

As I was lying in bed, not knowing what to do, my chihuahua, Duke, was beside me waiting to be fed. I'd had Duke for many years, and when I was travelling, my mom looked after him. He was my first baby and such a sweet dog that slept with me every night. I couldn't get up, let alone feed him. I somehow was able to get my cellphone that was charging beside me. I called my brother Mike as he was getting ready for work. I cried to him, explaining how I couldn't move and was so scared. He came over as fast as he could, picked me up out of bed and carried me to his car. I was like a dead weight. I was terrified once again as I had no idea what was going on with my body. I thought perhaps it was a result of the B12 deficiency and the nerve damage I had potentially caused from not eating properly. The lightning bolts through my body got worse and worse. As my brother drove me to the emergency room, I wailed with every bump in the road. I felt like my body was in a storm and the sharp, shooting pains were going to be the end of me. The tingling was all through my arms and there was numbness all through my back and neck. It was a very scary feeling. We got to the ER and my brother picked me up and carried me into the hospital waiting room and checked me in. I was sitting in the seat in so much pain with tears running down my face uncontrollably. They came and put a neck brace on me as I waited. Finally, they put me on a stretcher and brought me to the exam room. I lay flat waiting for a doctor for what seemed like an eternity. When the doctor eventually came, he seemed unfazed by my situation. He asked what happened. I said nothing. I woke up like this. Then he asked if I had done anything physical the day before. I explained that I'd done an aerial act a week prior, but I had no pain afterward. He asked if I had been under a lot of stress, and I said yes. I was always under a lot of stress. He said that often these types of nerve pains are caused by stress.

I eventually had an MRI and it showed that I had some damage to a disc in the vertebrae and the shift had caused some nerves to flare up. It made sense that this was nerve-related because my entire body was affected. I asked the doctor if he was sure this wouldn't escalate and lead to any form of paralysis. I told him I was going on tour and about to bend in half performing every night. He assured me it wouldn't cause paralysis (although he couldn't guarantee it) and told me to limit my stress and the number of hours I spent at a computer. He felt that the show I did out of the blue had shocked my body, and combined with the highly stressful week at my computer, my ligaments were under pressure and caused a shift in my neck that resulted in nerve pain. He mentioned that for people with extreme flexibility like me, these occurrences are common. As athletes, our joints are accustomed to a certain amount of activity and conditioning, and without strength training, if you're only flexing the joints, they can become loose and shift around. It was scary to think that at any moment this could happen again. The doctor gave me some pain medication and I was sent back home to rest and alternate with heat and ice to calm the nerves.

The pain medication worked, and I began to take a cocktail of muscle relaxer, Tylenol 3, and Naproxen. I was grateful to have the medication for the first few days, but of course they didn't agree with my stomach ulcers. I continued with just the muscle relaxer, which seemed to take the edge off, and I was able to return to work. I had lots on my plate, so this out-of-nowhere injury really threw me for a loop. I started to be a lot more conscious of my posture, especially when typing at my laptop.

David and I headed to Los Angeles together to attend Robert's star-studded wedding on July 31. The week before the wedding was so full of events that I rarely got to relax and spend quality time with him. Granted, David was easygoing and completely fine to relax in the hotel, but I felt bad because I worked the entire trip. Mixing work and pleasure sometimes adds a whole other level of stress. I felt guilty while I was trying to pull off so many events and have them all go off without any glitches. My hat is off to wedding planners. I couldn't fathom the thought of ruining a bride's wedding day.

Robert's wedding was a success — I'll leave it at that because of the non-disclosure agreements — and David and I headed home to Toronto for some downtime and to make plans for after the tour. That August was one of the best summer months of my life. We went to music festivals, hung out with friends, and attended a few weddings and birthdays. Granted, I was still working like crazy, but I did make time for the important things in life that pertained to my social life. And yes, I took care of my health.

The summer ended and I was excited, nervous, and sad to leave David for the tour. We had made plans to see each other throughout, but I knew the next three weeks I would have my head down, focused on creating the live show with the Rio Olympians. It was to be an amazing tour, because the U.S. women's gymnastics team took home the gold in the team and individual all-around, and the men had also done very well. There were lots of medals and records to celebrate and superstars like Simone Biles to showcase. I set off, ready to rock and roll and create a spectacular event.

I also felt I had my health under control when the tour began. My ulcers were better, and I made sure not to have an empty stomach when I took medication. I was taking my B12 supplements, and my neck hadn't flared up again. I did lots of strength training and stretching to prepare my body as best I could. I was in a good place mentally as well. I always feel a lot better when I have a purpose. If I'm not happy with my work, it really affects me mentally. I think it comes from my father and setting goals from a young age. I always need something to strive toward and look forward to. I can't do the same thing every day or live a status quo life. I push myself to my limits to achieve greatness. Sometimes I ignored my health along the way, but I was trying to do better this time around. And given what was about to happen on the tour, it was a wise move on my part.

○

Total darkness. I'm in the silk, curled up in a ball while I watch the act finish below me. Because I'm also creative director, I take mental notes, things to tell the performers once the show is over. Then it's my turn. "The Sound of Silence" starts to play, and my act begins. I fly twenty and thirty feet in the air, performing intricate contortions to the music, soaring above male gymnasts on the arena floor while they perform their routine. Everyone loves it. But my winch operator's timing is off. I'm not on the ground when I should be. I'm overlapping with the gymnasts below. I'm irritated that the winch operator isn't following my cues. I try to direct him, to signal to him as I'm midair. But he either isn't paying attention or he's ignoring me. I come to the most dangerous point in the act where I perform a trick some thirty feet in the air. I pull myself into a chin-up position, lift my legs above my head. I'm completely upside down. I hook my feet through the silk and release both arms so I can slide down the silk to my waist and do side splits to catch myself. As I slide, I once again try to direct the winch operator to go faster because he's completely off in the cues. I'm not paying attention to my routine, and I miss my mark. I am twenty feet above the stage when I lose control and fall. I can't do anything but wait for the bang.

O

September 2016. I arrived at the Colorado Olympic Training Center to put together the show. The facility had dorms, cafeterias, physiotherapy, and everything we could possibly need so we could focus on the task at hand. Many of the athletes had already trained there, so it was a very comforting place to be. I had special equipment made for the show, which was also being delivered to the facility, so we could figure out what exactly we would do with it. It was vital to showcase high-level gymnastics, but I also wanted to push the artistic boundaries of the gymnasts, because the audience would never expect them to manipulate a foreign prop or fly in the air on a circus apparatus. The audience was used to seeing them on their gymnastics equipment, but not hanging from the Olympic rings twenty feet in the air, or on a tiny strap smiling and waving. This was my favourite part of being a creative director, transforming these world-class athletes into circus performers. And as had been the case on the 2012 tour, in 2016 my fifth life as a solo aerialist and my sixth as a creative director/choreographer were about to mix in spectacular fashion.

Joining the 2016 tour was the "Final Five" gold medal–winning women's gymnastics team that included: Simone Biles, all-around individual Olympic champion; Aly Raisman, two-time Olympian and captain; Gabby Douglas, also a two-time Olympian; Laurie Hernandez; and Madison Kocian. We also had Nastia Liukin and Shawn Johnson to add to our star-studded cast. On the men's side, we had fan favourites Jake Dalton, Chris Brooks, Sam Mikulak, John Orozco, and Alex Naddour, who had won the individual bronze medal on pommel horse. To say this tour was set up to be a success would be an understatement.

We also had talented dance choreographers that John Macready had hired. They were amazing at pulling the best out of the gymnasts. I remember coming off my Olympic appearance and joining the Tour of Champions in 2004 and just being so burnt out that the thought of learning new choreography and working hard again was a challenge. I felt for the gymnasts because we asked so much from them on a choreographic level. They managed to push through their pain and exhaustion, as I had done, and learned incredible dances.

For my solo routine, I put together an aerial act on a piece of equipment I had never worked with before. On the 2012 tour, I had done an aerial rope act that I had developed at Cirque du Soleil, so I had to step it up a notch for 2016. One of the specially designed pieces of equipment I had made for the show was an "aerial bubble," which was essentially a glass ball that opened and closed, and I performed contortion inside it. My vision for the act included other rhythmic gymnasts performing in clear plastic bubbles on the floor. I always thought outside the box and this act was a big risk. USA Gymnastics had invested a lot of money in this number, so I had to make sure it wowed the crowd. I remember the first day when the aerial bubble arrived and got hooked up and was hanging a few feet off the ground, everyone was staring at me, waiting for me to perform. John came over and asked me how it felt. Given that I'd never attempted to do an act inside such a contraption, I joked, "I better YouTube 'how to perform inside a giant bubble.'" He laughed, but admired that I had the confidence to have this equipment made with zero experience in it. This was something I was good at, challenging myself to the next level of whatever it was I was working on. I perform best under pressure, so knowing the premiere was around the corner and I was to debut this act gave me the push I needed to create something beautiful and visually impressive.

Having said that, admittedly the bubble number was a little touch-and-go, but I stayed back after the long days of training to work on it, and it all came together. I also had a company manufacture metal 3D cubes for a transitional piece to give the male gymnasts a breather during their high bar flying act. The cubes would be manipulated by rhythmic performers, myself included. It did aggravate my neck, since the cubes were quite heavy. But that wasn't all, in addition to the bubble aerial and 3D cube acts, I was also going to be suspended high in the air in a silk hammock and on straps for the finale.

Silks are often seen in the circus; they resemble silk curtains but are much longer and hang from thirty feet in the air. This silk was in a U shape so I could lie in it and perform contortion skills. To make this happen, I worked with a technical crew member known as a winch operator, who controlled how high and how fast I could go. Essentially, my life was in the hands of the winch operator. I wasn't very strong at this point, so I had to make sure most acts were contortion-focused. This was my favourite number of the tour. I was centre stage doing the aerial hammock silk number in unison with the men's "rings" number to the song "The Sound of Silence." It was so powerful that it gave me goosebumps.

During each gruelling rehearsal day, I was simultaneously on my phone working for Robert, and if I had to open my laptop to send a calendar invite, I quickly did so at the side of the stage. It was crazy of me to juggle both jobs, now that I look back. I was trying to remember that I needed stability after the tour was over and that was why I was keeping up with my executive assistant work, but it almost made me have a nervous breakdown. I could feel that dull aching pain in my stomach, because instead of resting and going to eat on breaks, I was catching up on emails. Really, it was insane but as I look back now, I'm glad I did both. Even if my health (again) was starting to deteriorate.

We got through the rehearsals and were ready for the dress rehearsal. All the big guns were there to bear witness: Steve Penny, the CEO of USA Gymnastics, who had hired me for both tours, and various members of the board and Olympic Committee. They always vetted our shows because they wanted to make sure the gymnastics and artistry were at a high level and that the show flowed well. I would say the dress rehearsals were more pressure than premieres. Dress rehearsals are to test the waters, and if the big guns aren't happy, well it's back to the drawing board, and a lot of changes are necessary in a short amount of time before the premiere.

We warmed up backstage, some in costume and some not, depending on if the leotards had arrived yet. We did our team handshake, where we huddled together, and we came up with something fun to chant to pump everyone up. Then, we were off to perform our tour of champions for the big guns.

The opening of the show went off perfectly and the big guns loved it. As the show continued, I took notes while warming up for my numbers. The lights and technical cues were off, but nothing that obvious to the untrained eye. Every beat of the music was timed with the lighting. If one part was off, it threw an entire act off. It was frustrating at times because not everyone in the technical crew had experience in live shows or at least putting one together this fast. I always struggled with trying to give them constructive criticism or just flat out tell them when they got it wrong. I found that as a young director, and a female, these hot-headed men who had been in the industry a long time didn't like taking direction from me. I didn't care, because I was responsible for the success and overall impact of the show. Either they listened and made the corrections or could leave. As a woman, I learned very early on that you can't be nice in all situations. Men don't react well to soft women in power. So I always put on my director hat and told it like it was.

Then it was time for me to get ready for the "The Sound of Silence" routine with the aerial silk hammock and men's rings. This act had a fear factor, because while one act was finishing on the floor, I got ready in the silk, curled up in a ball, and got hoisted about fifty feet in the air in pitch black. I stayed in that ball in midair for about two minutes before starting my performance. This is another part of live entertainment. When one act is going on, the other acts are preparing, and often with aerialists, this means hanging in midair with no safety wire, alone, quiet in the dark. It is a little unnerving. Regardless, it was necessary for this part of the show to be a surprise. Aerial always requires your full attention. Even if you think you have it in the bag, when you get too comfortable is when you should be worried. I doubt that the pilot of a plane is ever comfortable flying through the skies. It's the same with aerial, you always need to be on your game with full attention.

The act began and the crowd was loving it, but now we are back to where this chapter began. My winch operator's timing was off. I tried directing him as I performed high in the air. It wasn't going well. Then the point arrived in the act where I was upside down thirty feet in the air and was about to slide down using my feet, hands free, in a risky move where I did side splits to catch myself. All of this was meant to wow the audience.

I should have focused on myself and not been so obsessed with perfection. But that's not who I am, so I continued trying to direct the winch operator, urging him to go faster. I missed my mark and couldn't save myself with my hands. I was twenty feet in the air when I lost control and fell. I remember it all in slow motion. I was falling headfirst toward the ground, thinking *this isn't happening, this isn't happening.* Well, it was, and I landed directly on my head. My feet went over my head, and I heard a crunching sound. I sort of rolled out of it and lay there on my back staring at the ceiling with the silk dangling above me. I heard gasps from the small crowd. I tried to get up right away, but John rushed over and told me not to move. I thought I was fine and could just walk it off. I could not. More and more people swarmed around me. Everyone kept repeating not to move. So I laid there, lifeless, but I could still feel my fingers and toes. By now the house lights were on. My vision started to blur, my head pounded from the impact, and the left side of my neck stiffened up. I felt tingly all over. Everyone looked at one another as if they knew something I didn't. The doctor on site checked my vitals and asked me questions, while John knelt beside me. "Do you know where you are?" "How old are you?" and "What is your name?" I believe I answered everything, but I honestly don't remember.

Eventually, it was decided that I didn't need a stretcher and the doctor and John helped me to sit up. When I did that, the entire arena started to spin. They asked how I felt, and being the athlete and performer I was, I lied. "I'm fine," I told them. I wasn't going to admit that I felt like vomiting, and I could barely see because the room was blurry and spinning. John clearly suspected I was hiding the truth, because he continued asking me questions until I finally snapped, "I'm fine, stop asking me questions." But he knew me well enough to know I wasn't fine.

The doctor helped me to stand. I could walk. I could very well have been paralyzed from that moment onward, but I wasn't. By the grace of God, I could walk. I made my way off the stage and sat in the stands. The tour doctor didn't leave my side, which I found annoying. I wanted to be left alone to reflect on what the hell happened. They don't call circus acts "death-defying" for no reason. I had plummeted twenty feet, almost to my death. Never in my career had I taken a fall like that. I'd fallen and gotten injured for sure, but never from that height, or while upside down, and not straight on my head without my hands landing first. It scared me. I didn't tell anyone, not even John, but I was terrified.

I watched the rest of the show from the stands and pretended to take my notes and act normal. Horrifyingly, as the show went on, I began losing vision in my left eye. It was going black, and I didn't have any peripheral vision. My right eye was fine, but my left eye, complete darkness. For that matter, the entire left side of my head all the way down my neck into my left arm and all the way to my pinky finger was tingling and painful. I knew I had a massive concussion, but was convinced I had to keep it to myself.

As the performance continued, my back started to spasm and my hips were aching. When I landed, my hips and back overstretched when I crunched in half. I still didn't know what the crunch noise that I heard when I landed was, and I preferred not to guess. But I think it may have been my back or hips. Whatever it was, it became very uncomfortable to even breathe.

On the upside, the show looked fantastic, even though we skipped over the parts I was meant to be in. The doctor was constantly talking to me throughout, but I tried to focus on the show, even though I could barely see my pad of paper. The doctor knew I wasn't myself. She knew very well I had a concussion. But I still wouldn't admit it. As the show finished, I applauded, and the president and board members all seem pleased. Steve Penny came over to check on me. "You gave everyone a scare," he said. "You need to focus on the task at hand, and if that means you should only direct and not perform, that's fine by me."

But I knew he wanted me to perform, because the circus part of the show added a lot of depth. "I'm totally fine," I lied again. "The show must go on."

USA Gymnastics always had a "push the gymnast to the limit" mentality back in the day. So I think for me to have nearly fallen to my death and to tell him I was fine made him proud of me. We are athletes, we are tough, and we don't complain. That was how I was taught to deal with pain or trauma. It was also how things were at Cirque du Soleil. I didn't know any other way to be.

While we gave the notes to the cast, the doctor was still glued to my hip, and I started to get even more annoyed. I smiled and tried to make sense of what I was saying and to act normal. My brain was fuzzy, and I was basically blind in the left eye and the tingling was getting worse. It also didn't help my "I'm fine" assertion that by this point I was also finding it difficult to speak. It was like I could think of what I wanted to say, but it was difficult to enunciate the words. The doctor wouldn't give me any pain meds because it was important that I relay all my symptoms. Which I wasn't. Regardless, we all huddled, put our hands together, and did our chant.

As I walked away, the doctor said to me, "I know you're not feeling well and you're not yourself." I assured her I was fine, just a little shaken up and sore, and was going to go rest and have a shower. She told me to call her at any hour of the night to report if my symptoms got worse. I gave her a hug and walked away. I was sure as hell not fine. I walked straight to the dressing room bathroom and collapsed near the toilet. I was convinced I was going to throw up. I had been holding in all my symptoms for hours. It all came to a head, and I threw up. I immediately felt a bit better. I just sat there trying to collect myself, because I couldn't break down yet. I still had to debrief with John and the technicians. I don't really remember that debrief other than I just rushed through it and as I was walking back to the dorms, John said to me, "You okay, Mary?

I thought I was going to be looking down at my friend when I saw her for the rest of my life." He was referring to looking down at me as if I were in a wheelchair. It struck a chord with me, and it took everything in me not to burst into tears. Like I had the doctor, I assured him I was fine and merely needed to get some rest. I made it to my dorm room, shut the door behind me, dropped my bag, and fell to the floor sobbing. I was hysterical and could barely breathe. I couldn't see out of my left eye, my entire body felt like a truck had hit me, and I was having difficulty breathing. I was in very bad shape. The premiere was only a few days away and tomorrow was a full day of rehearsals. I was the director and couldn't take a day off. I eventually got off the floor, ran myself a bath, and tried to calm down. I was in shock, I think, and it all needed to come out.

I got into the bath and continued to cry. Then I tried to lie there and breathe. I felt faint and nauseous and like I was going to black out. I knew that it wouldn't be good to black out in the bath. So I sat up and wouldn't let myself lie down because I was very faint. I was scared to fall asleep. I was worried that I wouldn't wake up. I was traumatized and didn't know what to do. I called David while I was in the bath to keep me distracted so I wouldn't pass out and so someone knew where I was just in case. David was so worried and wanted me to come home or tell someone how I was really feeling. I couldn't and I wouldn't even let him tell my mom. I just needed him to know where I was and if the line went quiet to call someone. I also wanted to hear his voice, because at that moment I felt more alone than ever. I couldn't tell anyone how I was truly feeling because it would jeopardize the entire tour. We still had a long way to go, and if I couldn't perform, there would be about fifteen minutes of the show missing, and it wasn't like I could train someone else to replace me in time. There were too many people relying on me, and I couldn't do that to the gymnasts that had worked so hard to be there. These gymnasts were tough as nails, performing with broken bones. I needed to be strong for them as well. Talking to David and lying in the bath letting my sore body recover helped. I was able to catch my breath and close my eyes and breathe. My panic attack subsided, and David called me every hour that night to make sure I was okay and not sleeping deeply. I guess after a concussion you're not supposed to go into deep sleep because you might not wake up or something. I really didn't know and didn't want to. I appreciated him checking in on me and making sure I was okay. After all, he was the only one who knew the truth.

The next morning, I was so stiff I could barely get out of bed. My ribs, back, and hips felt out of place. I felt like someone had beaten me with a baseball bat. My head was very bruised on the left side and my neck was so stiff I could barely look to the left. But none of that mattered in that moment because I could see out of my left eye again. Not entirely, since it was still glossy and blurry, but it wasn't black. I could make out colours and shapes, and I could read the emails that I had missed the day before due to my accident. The fact that my vision was back was a miracle. That was all I cared about in that moment. I knew that God and my guardian angel had watched over me and healed the part of my brain that was causing my temporary vision damage. I couldn't have gone on without the vision in my left eye. That is something I absolutely couldn't hide or fake for more than that one day I had to. I popped some muscle relaxer I had from when I threw my neck out back home and some painkiller I had brought. I felt almost instant relief, put my makeup on, tried to get dressed while flinching in pain, looked at myself in the mirror, and put on a brave face. I knew everyone would be looking at me and asking how I was, so I needed to appear like I was completely fine. I wasn't, but I was going to be. I just needed time to heal. I think what ultimately saved me was the fact that I was so flexible. When I hit the ground, my body literally folded in half. I didn't try to fight the fall, I let my body contort on landing and absorb the impact. I think if I had stiffened up, the outcome would have been much worse.

We carried on with rehearsals, but I didn't attempt my aerial act. Instead, I worked on my acts on the ground and modified certain parts of the show. I realized after the accident that I wasn't in the shape I needed to be in to perform such risky skills. I needed to perform skills the audience would enjoy and not death-defying skills that maybe wouldn't even be noticed. I didn't need to prove anything to anyone, so I watered down my aerial acts a little. The show was coming together beautifully. It was the best tour John and I had ever created, and we were so proud of it and couldn't wait for the official premiere.

During the last few days of rehearsal, some legal authorities came to visit. There was an ongoing investigation at the time that I didn't know too much about, but I knew it involved all our top female athletes. One by one, they were pulled from rehearsal and taken into a room to give statements. Eventually, I was pulled aside by our security team, and they filled me in on what was happening. It was an investigation into Larry Nassar, the sports doctor that had worked for USA Gymnastics during multiple Olympic cycles. I had heard rumors about him and that he had resigned because of allegations of sexual assault. The security team proceeded to tell me that hundreds of women had testified against Larry Nassar, then they asked me if I had any encounters that felt inappropriate with him during physio sessions or outside the gym. I was in shock. I was also still foggy from my fall and the concussion that I was secretly trying to recover from, but the 2012 incident immediately came to mind. I hadn't thought about my disturbing physio session with Larry since it had happened. I had pushed it away into an "out of sight, out of mind" category, convincing myself that I must have misinterpreted the therapy. I paused for a moment when asked if I had any incidents to report, and said I did. I told them what happened. How I was positioned to face a wall in a room full of people and how he put his hand up my sports bra and fondled my breasts while correcting my rib. I told them in detail what he did and how I felt uneasy afterward and knew that it wasn't right, but the only thing that mattered at the time was fixing my rib, which he did. I told them I never reported it, because I told one person on the tour right after, and they laughed it off, so I felt no one would believe me. I was also scared to report such an accusation, given my status as director of the tour. I didn't want to hurt my chances of ever being hired again by USA Gymnastics, since these tours meant everything to me. I also didn't want to tarnish my name or the sport of rhythmic gymnastics in any way, so I just kept quiet and brushed it under the rug. Only in that moment, in speaking to our security detail, did I realize I wasn't alone. They told me some of the stories the other athletes had come forward with, and I was so sickened. I thought to myself, *Why didn't I report this sooner? I could have saved so many athletes from Larry Nassar's abuse.* They assured me I wasn't the only one who was scared to speak out. The authorities already had more than enough testimony to put him behind bars for life. I asked if they needed my testimony on file, or if I needed to go public with my statement, and they said no, because of the many that had come forward before me. I also felt that my incident didn't even come close to the pain and suffering others endured, and I didn't want to take any attention away from their trauma. They deserved every ounce of recognition for their bravery and for surviving this horrendous abuse. I told the security team to reach out to me if the authorities wanted me to come forward, and that was the end of my direct involvement.

I was glad I finally spoke out, but I don't believe I intentionally held back this information. I honestly just never thought about it again after it occurred. That was a downfall of my personality. I was very good at going through traumatic experiences, getting through them, and burying them. I had lived through many hardships in my life, and never saw counsellors or sought help to talk through my emotions. As a gymnast, I was always taught never to cry or show weakness. So that's what I carried through into my personal life. It was at this moment I realized that perhaps I had swept a few too many experiences in my life under the rug, and it was time to face up to them and the underlying hurt I carried with me every day. But now wasn't the time to do that. I couldn't break a few days before the premiere, but it did feel good to tell someone about what had happened to me at the hands of Larry Nassar in 2012. Years later, on January 24, 2018, Larry Nassar was sentenced to a maximum of 175 years in prison for the sexual assault of minors. He had hurt so many girls and women, altering their lives forever, and he deserved his fate.

The day of the premiere finally arrived. We had made some last-minute tweaks and the performers adopted them all perfectly. With the media frenzy surrounding the "Final Five" women and the authorities visiting our tour taking statements, I was in awe of their strength, and I knew the crowd would be on their feet giving standing ovations every night. Nastia and Shawn shined in their dance number, and of course every act involving the men's and women's teams were a hit. I was able to pull myself together for my aerial acts. However, I was experiencing some alignment issues. Besides the left side of my head still being very bruised, headaches and nausea lingered, and I was stiff in my neck and upper back, my pelvic area seemed out of alignment, and I could barely do splits. I think when I fell, and my legs went over my head, my entire core and pelvic area shifted and hadn't returned to normal. I did splits on a roller, trying to loosen out the joints or spasms, which looked very weird, I'm sure. I was terrified because doing the splits caused so much pain. My flexibility was all I had, since my strength wasn't the greatest. In any case, the pain in my pelvic and groin area was the least of my worries, and I was able to push through the show. The physiotherapists wouldn't work on me in those areas because of everything that was going on with Larry Nassar and the charges against him. I had to self-medicate and do my own physio a lot of the time because the gymnasts always took precedence (as they should), and I was hiding many of my injuries and symptoms so that I could continue as director.

As the tour went on, for the first time in my life, I started to develop a fear of flying. I think the fall was a sign from God to let me know that if I wasn't doing aerial work as my full-time profession, it would be too dangerous to pretend to pick up where I left off each time. This would be my last time coming out of retirement. It was a promise I made to myself and God. I prayed each night after the shows. I thanked God for keeping me safe and asked him to keep me safe the next night, and promised that I would retire from aerial performing after this tour. I meant it; I would never fly in a circus capacity again.

As the tour continued, we had many celebrities roll through. Gymnastics in America is huge, and many high-profile people brought their kids to see the show and wanted autographs from Simone, Aly, Nastia, Shawn, and the rest. I loved meeting everyone and it was always very rewarding when they told me how much they loved the performance. I mean, these were world-class actors who had a ton of experience, and they were telling me they loved my show. It was an honour. This show was my heart, and I was glad that all the hard work and sacrifice meant so much to so many.

Our last show was special. My mom came out for it, and I was so grateful to have her there. She was always my rock, and I knew I was so tired and burnt out that I needed some downtime with her. A mom just knows what their child needs, and I just needed her by my side at that exact point. She came backstage and just talked to me about anything and everything that wasn't tour-related to distract me. She helped me with my hair and gave me massages, since she knew my body was in shambles. The tour was very demanding from a contortion standpoint, and I didn't have time to condition or train. In all honesty, even if I'd had the time, I probably wouldn't have even done it. I needed sleep, not to physically exert myself. At times, my hips popped out, same with my shoulders. I felt too loose and too flexible. If that's even possible. I was doing a lot of shows bending in half, and not doing enough strengthening and conditioning between. Granted, building muscle can make you less flexible, so that's why rhythmic gymnasts and contortionists are long and lean. No muscles to get in the way or block you from putting your head on your butt.

The final show went perfectly. And so it was that our tour wrapped and everyone went their separate ways. I returned to Toronto and was happy, even relieved, to be back with my family and friends. David and I picked up where we left off and enjoyed a lovely Christmas together. I didn't have such a hard time making the transition to the real world this time because I was so grateful to have survived. Having the fall early on really shook me up, and being able to overcome those injuries, and go out and perform every night with no safety wire, took a lot out of me. Especially while working a full-time corporate job at the same time. For once in my life, I was happy to only be juggling one job and giving my body a well-deserved rest. I returned to the office, set up my desk again, and got to work while hanging up my aerial equipment for good.

The old adage that when one door closes, another one opens is certainly true in my life. But I had left the aerial soloist door half-open when I'd taken the job with Robert. And now, after my accident, it was time to close that door fully and walk through the next completely free.

## What I Learned

**Reason:** This year of my life was one where I lived three lives concurrently: Solo aerialist, choreographer/creative director, and entertainment executive. This meant I had plenty of reasons to get out of bed and thrive. I wanted to succeed at my new job in the corporate world, and also to pay attention to my health and personal life. I wanted to create the best gymnastics tour yet. Then after the accident, I had to survive and work through agony so as not to let the tour down.

**Reinvent:** I had never planned to enter the corporate world at the level I did, but it seemed to be God's plan for me to work with Robert Herjavec. I wasn't looking for this precise opportunity, but when presented with it, I dove in head first, and it's been an adventure ever since.

And I also learned throughout this time in my life that reinvention isn't only about professional choices. I learned to reinvent my life as a romantic partner, and to trust again. That's a big one.

Learning to take care of my health was also part of this reinvention. I'd spent my life not eating properly, not getting enough sleep, and pushing my body to its limits. Now, it was time to be good to myself and prioritize my health.

And finally, I said goodbye to one of my passions, aerial performing. My aerial work ended in a big way, with a near-death experience. But more often, changes come about with more subtlety, and you have to read the signs to decide. Saying goodbye to one part of your life can be painful, but it can also be liberating. For me, in this moment, retiring from "flying" was liberating.

**Right:** It was my right to quit performing. I could have continued, but I had made a promise to God, and later to David, that I would quit, and I did.

O

Lives Five and Six had come to a spectacular end. Life Seven, Mary the entertainment executive, was here to stay. Next up, Life Eight ...

# 8TH LIFE:

# WIFE & MOTHER

---

September 1, 2020. They lay me on the operating table and elevate it so that my feet are up in the air and my head is down. All the blood instantly rushes to my head, and I am nauseous and light-headed. I tell them how I'm feeling, so they give me medication to ease the discomfort. My husband comes in and sits beside me and does his best to comfort me. They ask me if I can feel anything from the waist down. I can, so they wait. A couple minutes later they ask again, and I give them the same answer. They tell me I need to take deep breaths and that I will only feel pressure. I'm feeling more than pressure, but they need to start before the epidural wears off. So they begin cutting. I feel them pulling at my skin and a sickening sensation of intense pressure. Then I feel their hands inside me. I can feel the obstetrician moving organs around to get to the baby. And I feel unimaginable discomfort. I know then that the anaesthetist had not done my epidural correctly and I am feeling way more than I should be. My eyes fill with tears, they drip down my face and soak my mask. My husband wipes them dry and tries to help me breathe. The doctors and nurses keep telling me to relax. But I can't relax. The pressure, the pain, feels like it will never end. Eventually, they take my son out of me, and I hear him cry. They bring him around the curtain to show me. He is beautiful.

O

Three years earlier. Winter 2017. Despite hanging up my leotards and keeping my feet on the ground after leaving acrobatics behind, I was excited about my next chapter. I had come so far as a performer and had known the thrill of a live audience. But the time had come to live a calm and more peaceful life, and in one location. Even my job as Robert's executive assistant had settled down and I was travelling less often. An added bonus, working alongside one of the most successful businessmen in the world felt as though I had achieved a business degree. When you work that closely with a successful CEO, one who is truly multi-dimensional and who knows how to literally use every hour of a twenty-four hour day, day in, day out, you learn so much. I absorbed it all and became motivated to be better, do better, and I set very high expectations for myself. Again. If Robert believed in me, saw something in me, and trusted me, I needed to have the same confidence in myself.

On the personal front, David and I moved in together and began to discover what our future could look like. My condo was small, but we made it work for a short period. We still enjoyed the downtown scene and were going out with friends often. We needed time to be together for more than a few days without long periods of missing one another. Distance does make the heart grow fonder, but not if it's a continuous cycle of missing one another. I'd learned that the hard way during my years with Dominic while I was on tour with Cirque.

One of our newfound romantic traditions was that we headed to Niagara Falls, Ontario, on Valentine's Day, it was our thing to do when I wasn't travelling. Now that I was going to be home more, we still chose to keep the tradition. After the tour had wrapped up, David had wanted to go to Athens, where I had competed at the Olympics, but I didn't feel right about taking time off again. Robert had graciously allowed me to do the gymnastics tour, I couldn't ask for more time away from my desk.

Instead, we packed up the car and drove to Niagara Falls in February 2017, blasting music and feeling free. It was an incredible experience after the gruelling years I had endured, both mentally and physically. We checked into our hotel, which had a spectacular view of the waterfalls, and we popped champagne and began our weekend.

Niagara Falls is a romantic town. It truly is like a mini–Las Vegas. David and I went for lunch and walked along the boardwalk before eventually ending up at the Niagara SkyWheel, an enormous Ferris wheel that had become a major tourist attraction in the city. To my surprise, David wanted to take a ride, in fact he was eager to go on it, which shocked me because he was afraid of heights. He was absolutely terrified when he saw me flying on the tour. But he insisted. We bought our tickets and headed toward the entrance when David stopped suddenly and said there was a problem with one of the tickets and he asked me to hang tight while he went back to the counter. I thought that was strange, how could you screw up two tickets for a Ferris wheel? I waited and watched the people ahead of us enjoy the ride. Kids, teenagers, couples. These were all normal people, and they were doing normal things, and here I was, finally one of them. David returned and said we were all set. So we approached the Ferris wheel and climbed into the gondola, which was fully enclosed by glass, not one of those open-air ones. Still, David was shaking with nerves. I didn't realize just how afraid of heights he was until that moment. To me, the Ferris wheel and its enclosed gondola felt safe compared to flying hundreds of feet in the air with no safety wire. Regardless, I appreciated him planning such a special day for us.

As we went around and around, I tried to make conversation and take pictures, but David was clammed up and nervous. His nerves only grew worse when the Ferris wheel stopped without warning, with our gondola right at the top. I thought, *Oh man, David is going to die being stuck up here.* It didn't really faze me because I was accustomed to technical glitches during Cirque, when I would be suspended for thirty minutes until they corrected the programming errors. I laughed to myself, even in my normal life I couldn't escape these malfunctions. As I looked out at the scene, David finally opened his mouth and spoke, "Mary."

I turned and there he was, on bended knee in the little gondola high in the sky. I thought he was crazy for getting off his chair and kneeling in midair. He reached in his pocket and pulled out a jewellery box. My heart stopped; I was completely shocked. "Will you marry me?" were the next words out of his mouth. The gorgeous diamond ring was shining in the sun. He was still shaking on one knee, balancing himself in this little pod, and I immediately jumped at him and screamed, "YES!"

We both cried but agreed to sit back on our seats because we were making our little pod shake from our excitement. Then, just as suddenly as it had stopped, the Ferris wheel started again. I couldn't believe that David had planned the entire thing, including the stopping of the Ferris wheel. His claim that there was something "wrong" with our tickets was a ruse to ask the operator to stop it at the precise moment we were at the top. David put the ring on my finger, which of course fit perfectly. I also finally understood why he wanted to go away on a trip to Europe. He planned to propose where I competed in Athens. Yet despite my refusal to travel, David had pulled off an epic surprise. I was so happy, in love, and finally at peace. David was my soulmate, and he had just made me the happiest girl on the planet. When we exited our little pod, everyone began to applaud. It was all premeditated and I had no idea, and we were on cloud nine. It felt like a dream, like I was living in a fairy tale with no cares in the world. I loved it and was so excited to see what came next.

○

We chose our wedding venue and set a wedding date of June 30, 2018, which gave us a year to plan. We rented out the one-bedroom condo, said goodbye to our downtown Toronto life, and moved north of the city.

Our wedding was perfect. I had family and friends fly in from all over the world. My brother Matt came from Rome, where he was working hard running a business empire. Colleagues from Los Angeles flew in, and other friends came all the way from New Zealand. We were overwhelmed by the outpouring of support and the number of people who made the effort to be in attendance.

My mother walked me down the aisle while I held my flowers. As a way to have my father with me, I had a photo of him dangling from the bouquet. I knew my father was there with me in spirit. It was very hard for Mom and me to keep it together, because she had been both parents to me ever since my father passed. As she walked with me, I could feel the years of hardship she endured to get me to this point.

Our wedding reception was a full-on stage event, but what else would anyone expect from a performer like me? Everyone entered with a dance and a song that they had chosen. To surprise David, I had secretly practised a dance along with my bridal party and mom and aunt. Initially, I wasn't planning on doing any performance of my own considering that, as the bride, the whole event had me in the spotlight. But Debra Brown, the Cirque du Soleil choreographer, told me I *must* perform because that is who I am, and I would regret it if I didn't. At times I felt Debra knew me better than anyone. It was like she could see my soul and its longing to be onstage even after retirement. Once an artist, always an artist, I reminded myself. I thought long and hard about what kind of performance I would do. Debra sent me a song that put it all into perspective: "Love on the Brain" by Rihanna. That was the song I would use. Debra and I virtually choreographed the routine and I brought together my entire bridal party, as well as my mom and aunt. We came together only once to rehearse. However, it went off perfectly. We sat David in a chair front and centre and performed for him. He loved it. I used all my skills and didn't make any errors with my ribbon. I was so relieved. My mom and aunt were absolute superstars, and I was so proud to perform alongside them. I will always cherish that dance, and every time I hear "Love on the Brain," I think of that moment.

After the wedding we flew to Hawaii for our honeymoon. I still felt the island was magical, even though in 2004, prior to my *Vanity Fair* photoshoot, I had suffered the worst sunburn of my life there. It was a wonderful trip and set the stage for our marriage.

After our whirlwind year of moving, getting engaged, and getting married, David and I were looking forward to a quieter, simpler life. I never had a lot of stability or stillness in my life, so to experience that with him was something that thrilled me. This time would be different from my first marriage. I was a mature woman now, one who knew what she wanted. I was confident in who I was, and I could focus with David on making our marriage all we knew it could be. Just the two of us. Well, God had another plan. I got pregnant almost immediately following our wedding. And thus began what I consider my eighth life, that of wife *and* mother.

David and I had discussed wanting a family. I was worried that after all my years of abusing my body and with all the medications I'd taken to get through my days as an athlete and performer, I wouldn't get pregnant. My mother always assured me she was very fertile, and I shouldn't have any issues. I wasn't so sure because of the high stress, dieting, and medications. But she was right. I got pregnant in the fall of 2018 and our newlywed lives turned upside down.

I took about ten pregnancy tests. We were in shock. But I was thankful I had retired from performing and was comfortable in my corporate job, and we had settled into our new home. At least now all we needed to do was make a nursery. It felt like a lot to take in, but we felt very blessed that we were on this new journey. I saved the positive pregnancy tests for a few days until I went to the doctor for an actual blood test that also came back positive. It was official, we were pregnant!

David was with me every step of the way during my pregnancy, and I knew he was going to be the best dad. Since I had grown up without a father, I never wanted kids unless it was with the right person. I didn't want my children to have one parent, or parents in two different homes, if it could be avoided. David came from a traditional Italian upbringing, so family was very important to him. David always wanted kids and was waiting for the right time. Now was the time. He dove in right away and started to prepare our townhouse for the arrival of our baby without even being past the first trimester. I'm not sure you ever truly know when you're ready for kids. It just happens and your maternal instinct kicks in and you have this mini-me that is reliant on you 24/7.

We learned we were having a little girl, and that all the tests showed she was healthy. That's all we cared about. The changes happening to my body took some getting used to after years of me being in control of how it behaved and moved, but now my daughter was in charge. I also had placenta previa, which is a low placenta covering part of the cervix, so I wasn't necessarily on bed rest, but I wasn't allowed to work out, walk for long periods, or exert myself in any way. So keeping up with my social life or events was basically out of the question. I had to learn how to be lazy. Not an easy task for an overachieving Olympian circus acrobat!

I went to work and came home, lay on the couch, and David would do all the cooking and cleaning. My mother once told me a story about when she was cleaning the kitchen floor and went into labour as her water broke right then and there. I knew that genetically, if I overexerted myself, there was a chance of my water breaking or having the placenta detach, so I needed to listen to my doctor.

As for being lazy, given that I was tired all the time, my back ached, and my hips were very sore, I didn't have much choice but to rest. I was growing in all areas, and gained fifty pounds with this pregnancy. I weighed the most I ever had in my life. I tried not to weigh myself at home, but the obstetrician always weighed me when I arrived at the office to make sure the baby was growing well. I mentally had to convince myself this wasn't the time to worry about weight and dieting. But the truth was that I didn't recognize myself or who I had become. Everyone tells you that you are glowing and look beautiful, but I knew I wasn't myself and I felt gross. I didn't fit into anything, so my mom constantly sent me maternity clothes so I would be comfortable. I was used to my skin-tight jeans or short shorts, but that was no longer my reality. That's another thing that is rarely spoken of. When you become pregnant, the only support you have is your obstetrician, who weighs you and spends maybe fifteen minutes asking how you are and sends you home. I feel like the complete change in lifestyle is a shock and perhaps a bit of a secret society. Or perhaps my feelings were entirely due to being an Olympic athlete, and therefore accustomed to using my body as my profession for so long that being pregnant felt so foreign.

I continued to work throughout my pregnancy. I wore clothes that wouldn't make everyone immediately change the subject to the baby and tried to maintain some form of my fearless "go-getter" reputation. Looking back, I suppose I was trying to conceal it instead of embracing it. Perhaps other women in high-level careers feel the same way. You are looked at a certain way — as an ambitious, skilled, dedicated professional — and then, once you get pregnant, it's assumed that you no longer put your career first. It was a very difficult period in my career, because I felt like I was experiencing a lot of setbacks. I was up for a promotion but didn't get it. I was set to travel for some work trips, but they got pulled at the last minute. Many of my friends were living their fun social lives and I wasn't invited anymore. I felt as though getting pregnant made others forget about me or unconsciously press pause on me. Maybe it was for my own good, maybe it was all in my head, but it hurt at the time.

Despite all the setbacks and disappointments, I was reminded of the blessing I was growing inside me with every ultrasound. I had transformed and reinvented my life so many times, and in so many different ways, and now pregnancy was the next stage in my journey. From gymnast to Olympian to circus acrobat to aerialist to creative director and choreographer to executive assistant to a famous CEO, wife, and now soon-to-be mom, my life was a constant transformation, all before I was thirty-five years old. I loved reinventing myself and challenging myself to become the best version of myself (with many lessons learned along the way) and to continue accomplishing the unexpected. It was only the beginning and that's what helped me through my pregnancy.

David made sure the nursery was perfect and we were ready to welcome our baby girl. After two days of labour, she arrived. We named her Ava Jacilynne Rose after my mother and my husband's mother. She was beautiful and opened her eyes almost instantly.

She was ready to come into this world and was looking all around, exploring right from the start. She weighed seven pounds, eight ounces and was born June 5, 2019, at 11:47 p.m. I had her before midnight. Not even a year after our wedding. She stole her daddy's heart from the moment they locked eyes. I knew then and there I was no longer the only woman in his life, and I was fine with that.

Ava was a beautiful baby girl, but she had colic. It's most common during the first six weeks of life. It usually goes away on its own by age three to four months. Up to one in four newborn babies may have it. Lucky me, Ava was the one of the four. In any case, there wasn't much we could do but let her cry it out. I was pretty used to letting my emotions numb me due to my gymnastics training and having to just go on autopilot so often. My husband, on the other hand, had a very hard time tuning out the crying.

It was also a major adjustment learning to breastfeed, getting little or no sleep, and having a colicky baby. It hits you all at once and can become extremely overwhelming. I didn't tell anyone, but I was having some negative thoughts about myself and really didn't feel like I was in my own body. I felt loose, like my joints were out of socket half the time. I was heavy and had a lot of back pain and my pelvic muscles were nonexistent. On top of caring for a newborn, I just didn't feel right in my skin. Not to sound vain or selfish, but not feeling in shape or like myself really took a toll. During my pregnancy, I forced myself to ignore these feelings, and what had happened to the Olympic athlete's body. But after a few months without a baby inside of me, I expected my body to bounce back, and it just didn't. All those years of gymnastics and muscle memory didn't help all that much to return my body to its pre-pregnancy form. I tried to work out or go for walks, but then I felt a lot of groin pain and started bleeding again. It was frustrating. Here I was trying to care for a newborn who was always crying, trying to work out and do something for me, and then my health issues once again stopped me.

An offshoot of this period was how it changed my view of social media. I felt angry at the moms who were posting not even three weeks after having a baby with no stomach, fully in shape and running again. New moms who seemed to have no issues taking personal time and had makeup on every day and looked amazing. I was a mess, day in and day out. I ended up taking a break from social media to preserve my mental health.

Even after six months, I couldn't work out properly. I was tired of being told what I could or couldn't do. It was a tough year, and I had a bout of postpartum depression. Again, I never told anyone. My husband was at work, and I was home all day with Ava, and she cried and cried due to her colic. There were times when I just sat in her room while she cried in the crib, and I sobbed as well. I lost it a few times but did my best to hold it together. I felt like a car going full speed and never being able to slow down. I remember not being able to shower or brush my hair for days. On top of it all, I was still about thirty pounds heavier than my typical healthy weight. I had no time for myself. My husband tried to help, but newborn babies and their moms have a special bond. I breast-pumped as much milk as I could so my husband could feed Ava and give me a break, but then it only lasted so long. David rocked her in a small rotating chair and slept there with her on his chest so I could rest. He was a trooper, but we were hit hard with this newborn baby reality.

On top of the normal challenges of being a new mom, I was also working full-time. Robert had hired someone, but they didn't work out. I offered to continue working so I didn't have to go on the government maternity leave pension, because quite frankly, we needed more money than what it offered, since we were saving for our dream house and still paying off our wedding. It was absolutely insane of me to take that on, but hey, that's who I am. Pushing through boundaries and barriers constantly.

Newborn babies sleep a lot during the day, so it was manageable for the first few months. Granted, I didn't sleep because I was up all night feeding, but I could survive on no sleep because Ava slept most of the day. I really felt like I had everything under control. I started work early if she was sleeping, breastfed, played, breastfed, put her down for a nap, pumped, answered emails, maybe ate something before she woke up, breastfed, and repeated. That was the routine for Ava's first year.

My life had been spent changing and adapting with my career and anything else that got thrown at me. Especially performing live on stage, you always need to improvise if and when things don't go according to plan. It was good training for what happened next. I was out for a baby-shower brunch with friends in January of 2020. Ava was around six or seven months old at the time and I wasn't feeling well. All the food that was brought to the table made me feel ill. Not feeling 100 percent was a constant in my life and I always just pushed past it. But this time, I knew it was more than just exhaustion, I had felt this way before. I tried to smile and drink a Caesar that didn't go down well at all. I switched to water and had dry toast and tried to be present.

On the way home, I stopped at the pharmacy and grabbed a pregnancy test. This couldn't be happening again. My body was still healing, and I didn't feel like myself yet at all. I didn't think I could go through another pregnancy so soon. I drove home and the dizziness and nausea got worse. I had this feeling in my gut that I was pregnant again. My obstetrician had warned me. She kept asking what our birth control plan was because I didn't want to go back on the pill. I didn't want to be reliant on any form of prescription medication ever again. I got home and was greeted by David and Ava and tried to act normal. When I put Ava down for a nap, I sneaked off to take the pregnancy test. I was waiting for what seemed like an eternity. Sure enough, positive. I calculated the difference; our babies were going to be fifteen months apart. Two kids under two. What were we thinking! Well, we had no choice at this point, so off we were on another new journey. We had also taken the leap and bought a bigger home. We were going to need the space, that was for certain.

Again, my life never seemed to take a pause. From one profession to another, travelling constantly to settling down, even my new world was full of reinvention, changes, and adapting. I thought that settling down to have a family would be planned on my terms, but here I was again just chasing my life. Getting married in 2018 and having two kids by 2020 was not in the plan, but David and I were of course grateful. And I quickly realized that this was all God's plan. The challenging few years that had passed, as well as the challenging years ahead, were all what we were meant to do. It took a while, but I got there. It wasn't fair to my family to not be happy, so I made a conscious effort to embrace this pregnancy. And soon enough we discovered our second child was a boy.

O

Our new house had more space for Ava. She was becoming a toddler and could almost walk, which meant she needed constant stimulation. I was falling behind at work and having trouble juggling my job and taking care of Ava while being six months pregnant with our son. It's all a blur now, but somehow my years of discipline as a training Olympian was no doubt a factor in my ability to handle it all.

By then another seismic event hit that made life stand still for my family and everyone else's, the first wave of the Covid-19 pandemic, and we were in lockdown. We loved our new house, but we couldn't explore much. We were on house arrest and not able to go to playdates, jungle gyms, or anything else. My mom couldn't even help me because of the restrictions in place. I was in complete isolation as I battled some form of postpartum depression, while being six months pregnant and working full-time.

Every day was the same and I had to find ways to entertain Ava while feeling so empty inside. My tank was completely empty. That's how my mom would put it. If your tank is empty, you have nothing to give. That resonated with me. I was running on empty for months and months. I had some meltdowns and didn't know what to do. I needed to find a way to fill the tank a little each day. I started walking at first, which helped. Although soon enough, summer came around and I was eight or nine months pregnant and wasn't able to walk very much, especially while pushing a toddler in a stroller and getting overheated. So I found a new passion, writing.

I wrote down my ideas for television and film projects that I wanted to tackle one day. Where did this sudden urge to create stories come from? I had watched countless shows and movies since I was pregnant with Ava and practically on bedrest. I became inspired and thought, *Why not create content that I would like?* Writing became my escape. No matter how tired I was, I sat down and wrote. My tank slowly began to fill.

Ava's first birthday in June 2020 was a game changer. She had taken her first few steps a week or so before and it was almost like she needed to be free and not crawl everywhere. Ava was always an energetic and curious baby. She didn't have an attention deficit, but she needed to be stimulated constantly, and the pandemic was very hard for her. I used to take her to the mall just to be out and see people. There was also a play gym there that closed. Not being able to socialize with other kids or play was difficult for her. She didn't know any better, but I knew with her personality she would thrive being in daycare. Thankfully, restrictions loosened up a little, and my mom started to come down to my house for the day and play with Ava outside and take her for walks so I could get some work done and rest. The heat was too much for me and I was so pregnant that I couldn't do much. I could barely even lift Ava.

I also gained almost sixty pounds during this pregnancy and hadn't lost my baby weight from Ava. I broke the two hundred pound mark, which was a first for me and made me depressed. Everyone has their own ideal weight, but two hundred pounds was a metric I never in my life thought I would hit. My joints didn't do well with the extra weight, either. With my gymnastics injuries and carrying way more weight than my body was used to, I was miserable. However, I still ate my pie and ice cream in bed every night. It was a time in my life where I ate to compensate for being depressed. "Comfort eating" is the term.

Pregnancy, as beautiful as it is creating life, gave me major identity issues. It was like I was a different person during both my pregnancies. I became introverted and reclusive during my second pregnancy. Partially because of the pandemic and partially due to my appearance. I didn't want to be in photos unless I took them. I had also found out that my son was in breech position and I would probably need a Caesarean section. I didn't take the news lightly, because I had never been under the knife. With all my injuries as a gymnast and in Cirque du Soleil, as well as on the gymnastics tours, I had never broken a bone. I had ankle subluxations, slipped discs in my neck and back, turf toe, dislocated ribs, but never anything that required surgery.

My thirty-fifth birthday was at the end of August, and I was due for a C-section on the first of September. Leading up to that date, my obstetrician tried everything to naturally flip my son, but with no success, and the attempt was one of the most painful, unnatural experiences of my life. Every time the doctor tried to move my son, his heart rate significantly dropped, as did mine. My husband couldn't even watch while multiple doctors were elbow deep, pushing on my pregnant belly trying to manipulate my son. It felt so disgusting that I almost threw up multiple times. I told them to stop immediately. It didn't feel right, I was worried they would harm my son, which they assured me the procedure could not. But I couldn't see how constant pressure, pushing, and prodding on my belly wouldn't damage my baby. Defending my unborn child, I got up and told them we'd proceed with the C-section on the scheduled date. Even though I dreaded the thought of surgery, that was the reality. So David and I went home. But I could barely sleep that night due to the pain and bruising on my stomach, as well as the cramping I was experiencing. All the aggressive pushing and manipulating really took a toll on me and my son. Thankfully, the next morning I could feel him kicking away inside me. I felt bad for putting him through that ordeal, but I guess it was part of the journey.

My husband, daughter, and I went out for my thirty-fifth birthday to a patio, since only patio dining was available at this stage in the pandemic. I was extremely uncomfortable, but it was nice to be out. While my birthday wasn't anything very special, it was perfect for the state I was in. My mom came down a few days prior to my C-section to watch Ava and allow David to finish putting our son's crib together and to run some last-minute errands. It was an intense time and I tried to keep busy rather than focusing on the C-section.

The morning of the surgery arrived, and I was admitted. There were a lot of Covid-19 protocols that needed to happen prior to landing on the operating table. I also needed to be briefed on the procedure, have an ultrasound to make sure the baby was still in breech position, and have my vitals checked to make sure I was healthy enough to handle such an invasive surgery. My husband wasn't allowed in until the last moment because of Covid.

One of the first things the medical staff did was to give me an epidural to numb my body prior to operating. I'd had an epidural after thirty-six hours of labour for Ava, so I was familiar with what was required. However, the anaesthetist who gave me the epidural was not good. She poked and prodded my back with a large needle and couldn't seem to find the right spot. She kept telling me to be still while I bent over on the cold metal operating table and she continuously jabbed my back. The best way I could describe it is someone poking your funny bone over and over and telling you to stay still. It was clear she didn't know what she was doing, although she was an older person. I guess eventually she found the spot and the epidural was done, but I was already crying at this point from the discomfort of her multiple failed attempts.

Then, as I described at the opening of this chapter, I suffered through a horrible ordeal. Having the C-section without a proper epidural. It was hell. I didn't think I could get through it. But eventually, my son was born. He was beautiful. He had a perfect little face. My husband went with him while they weighed him and got to hold him before I could. My obstetrician told me that there was a knot in his umbilical cord, which had probably prevented him from flipping and caused his heart rate to drop when they were trying to turn him. The poor thing, while they attempted to flip him the knot only got tighter and made him strain. I knew that procedure was a failure, and I couldn't understand how they couldn't see the knot to begin with. Regardless, my son was delivered and was healthy and that's all that mattered.

We named him Gabriel David. I always loved the name Gabriel, like the angel, and thought Gabe for short was adorable. We chose David for a middle name after his father. He was seven pounds and two ounces and was born at 7:02 a.m. on September 1, 2020. He was such a little angel and gentleman from birth. Very calm and loving. He was already different from my daughter, and we shared a unique bond from the start. I found it fascinating how you can love your kids the same but have two very different bonds with them. I was a very lucky mother to have two beautiful children so close in age to one another. I hoped they would be best friends and experience only the best in life. David and I always said that we wanted to give our kids everything. Not every child is fortunate enough to have parents who can support their dreams, especially from a financial aspect, so David and I started saving and putting away funds the moment they were born. Whatever our kids wanted to be when they grew up, we would have the means to make their dreams come true.

I went home from the hospital twenty-four hours after Gabe was born. Typically, you should stay in the hospital for forty-eight hours, but I saw how uncomfortable my husband was on the tiny couch and my son was doing well, so I figured why lie there when I could lie at home? It was a bad decision.

Once I got home, debilitating migraines began. They were so bad that I couldn't get out of bed and care for Gabe. My mom and David had to bring Gabe to me so I could breastfeed him while lying down. Anyone who knows how hard breastfeeding is, especially in the first week with a newborn, will know that trying to do it lying down was not ideal. I struggled for a few days, not being able to sit upright because of the migraines. As soon as I lay down, the migraines stopped. My mom went online and researched postpartum headaches. And guess what the likely cause was? An error with an epidural injection, specifically that the anaesthetist may have punctured my spinal cord, causing fluid to leak. Remember, my mother had been a nurse, so she wasn't being hysterical, she knew this was an actual risk given my symptoms. I had to go to the hospital immediately.

All the way there, I was in tears. It was about a thirty-minute drive sitting upright and I felt like puking when we pulled up. I made my way inside with my head pounding. I could barely open my eyes. The hospital lights were too bright and made my migraine worse. When I eventually saw a doctor, he admitted me and ran some tests. He had me sit up and lie down over and over, and then he saw the multiple needle puncture wounds in my back where the anaesthetist had trouble getting the epidural needle in the right spot. I knew that the anaesthetist had botched my epidural, and this was the consequence.

The doctor explained to me that I had a spinal headache, which is caused by leakage of spinal fluid through a puncture hole in the tough membrane that surrounds the spinal cord. This leakage decreases the pressure exerted by the spinal fluid on the brain and spinal cord, which leads to a headache. So essentially, the fluid in my brain was leaking out of my spinal cord, causing my brain to dehydrate and bounce around with not enough fluid. My brain was like a fish out of water. My mother's internet search had been correct. And it all made complete sense to me. I literally felt like I had a house on my head when I was sitting upright, and was completely fine when I lay down.

The doctor was booked up the entire day with surgeries but said he would make time for me. I needed to receive an epidural blood patch. This meant injecting a small amount of my own blood into the space over the puncture hole. The goal was to form a clot to seal the hole, restoring normal pressure in the spinal fluid and relieving my headache. I was all for it, but essentially it meant I needed to undergo another procedure exactly like the epidural. They needed to draw my blood at the same time as injecting it into my spine in the exact area where the anaesthetist had jabbed me so many times. The doctor admitted that the anaesthetist had poked me so many times he would have to seal a few holes in my spine. Of course, all of this came with many risks. Then he started to list them for me: I could end up paralyzed, endure chronic pain in my lower extremities, or experience dizziness, vertigo, tinnitus, and rebound intracranial hypertension. I had to ask him what that was in real people talk. Apparently, it means that the pressure of the fluid that surrounds the brain is too high, which can cause two problems, severe headache and visual loss. If left untreated, I could end up with permanent visual loss, even blindness.

Essentially, the procedure could leave me with even more problems than the migraines I was suffering from. I wasn't sane at the time, so thankfully my husband arrived, and I asked him to make the decision for me. He said that I couldn't go on in the pain I was currently in, and I was healthy otherwise, and that the risks were a worst-case scenario like all procedures or surgeries have. The doctor was confident that I would be fine, and I liked that about him. He put me at ease.

To be honest, this whole episode felt like another segment in a never-ending saga of setbacks, but hopefully this was the last hurdle. The doctor began poking and prodding my already very sore back and it hurt like hell. I was hunched over a pillow, sitting up with my head pounding. I'm not sure what hurt more at the time, my head or the doctor jabbing more needles in my spine. It was gruelling. But I desperately needed this to work, I couldn't go on in such pain and raise two kids. When the procedure ended, I was told to lie down very slowly. I had to stay there and not move for two hours to let the blood they inserted into my spine scab over the holes in my spinal membrane.

I dozed off during those two hours. I was so tired and needed to sleep off the tumultuous last few days. Nurses came in periodically to make sure I wasn't moving. The whole procedure could go down the drain if I moved. I had no intention of repeating that procedure, so I lay motionless until the doctor came back in. He told me it was the moment of truth and I needed to sit up. I was terrified to try, I wanted to lie there peacefully with no pain forever. I didn't know what I'd do if the migraines returned. I knew I would never leave the hospital this time if I wasn't fixed. Thank God when I sat up, I wasn't dizzy. The doctor, nurses, and my husband stared at me as if I was an alien. It was as though they had all placed bets on whether I would be okay or not. But I had no headache. They turned the lights on, and I could open my eyes and not have to squint. I started to tear up out of joy, and pandemic or not, I hugged the doctor tightly and thanked him with all my being. He apologized for the setback I had endured on behalf of the anaesthetist and said he would be sure to investigate it. I thanked him because I never wanted another new mother to have to endure this pain. It could have been avoided if my epidural had been performed correctly. Anything dealing with the spinal cord is so serious, and I was relieved that this doctor knew the risks and severity of spinal headaches.

We went home at last, and I was able to hold and breastfeed my son for the first time in peace. I was a new woman, and my husband was so relieved. He was so worried, stressed, and exhausted. He was my rock, and I was so grateful for him. I even played with my daughter before her bedtime. It felt like ages since I could smile and be present with her. For only being fifteen months old, she was such a strong little girl, and she immediately took on the protective sister role. She loved her brother Gabe from the start and would never let anyone come near him unless she said so or had given him a hug. I think Gabe is very lucky to have a sister like her.

The next morning, I woke up afraid to sit up for fear that my migraines would return. My mom had greeted me in bed with a very strong triple iced espresso drink because she read that after the blood patch procedure, it's good to stay heavily caffeinated to prevent the headaches from returning and constrict the blood vessels leading to the brain. I sat up and had a dull headache, nothing debilitating, but I could tell that some fluid was still leaking from my spine. This was probably what typical minor spinal headaches felt like, and it was nothing compared to the migraines I had previously experienced. Still, worried they would return, I had five to eight of those caffeinated drinks per day and it helped minimize my headaches. I wasn't a coffee drinker, but I knew it was only temporary.

Throughout all of this, I was taking painkillers for the C-section. I wasn't supposed to lift anything or strain in any way. It was difficult to follow those orders with a fifteen-month-old and a newborn. All the medications with the exorbitant amounts of caffeine took a major toll on my stomach, and the ulcers that I had tried to keep under control brought the dull ache in my stomach back. I knew it was my ulcers, but I tried to eat a lot and I would deal with that after I had healed more.

By now, my daughter had started daycare and was loving it. My mother had returned home, and I was juggling work and my newborn son. At times it was lonely, but I didn't have the same mental struggles or postpartum depression as I did with Ava. I think having gone through it once, now being in our forever home, and already being used to staying home through a maternity leave and pandemic, it wasn't as big an adjustment for me.

I also had an epiphany after Gabe. I was done having kids. I spoke with David, and he felt the same way. We had our son and our daughter, and we were content. We never wanted to be outnumbered. I have no idea how my mom endured having three children under three and later raising us all as a single parent. Having two with my husband's support was tough. Regardless, while I was home with my son, I had a flow of ideas and concepts flooding my brain. As I had when Ava was born, I began to write them down, and soon realized what the next chapter of my ever-evolving life and career would be. Life Nine would involve creating content in all forms.

## What I Learned

**Reason:** Motherhood is perhaps the most important reason, certainly the most experiential, I ever had for getting out of bed. Children are humbling, loving, and a blessing.

**Reinvent:** I can't say being a new mom was a reinvention like my previous lives, but it certainly was an eye-opener! But learning how to cope through postpartum depression, health challenges, and my own body image issues, was a kind of awakening in acceptance.

**Right:** It was my right to admit that motherhood wasn't enough for me, and recognizing it, and acting on it doesn't make me a bad parent. If anything, it makes me a better parent because my children can witness their mother achieving more dreams in front of their young eyes. My children have even inspired me to write a children's book. Stay tuned.

O

Life Eight, wife and mother, were full-time jobs, but there was more to come. Next up, Life Nine …

# 9TH LIFE:
# WRITER, ACTOR, PRODUCER

---

April 2021. The makeup artist finishes with a dab of face powder. After years of doing my own hair and makeup for Cirque, this feels decadent. I look in a mirror. Reflected back at me is a polished, confident woman. Inside is closer to the truth, I'm extremely nervous, with a stomach full of butterflies as I recite my lines in my head over and over. Today is my first time on set, and my first acting role. I still have a lot of baby weight from both pregnancies. Despite not feeling good about my body, I vow to act confident because my character, a sports commentator named Brianna Alcroft, is extremely confident. I squeeze into a tight red shirt and black slacks and a third assistant director walks me to set. The props person gives me a microphone to hold as I "interview" the young gymnast character. Years of live performance come in handy as I put every negative emotion and insecurity aside. I do five takes and nail my lines each time. Everyone applauds and I hear crew members say they can't believe the shot is done so quickly. It had to be fast because I'm not only an actress on set, I'm also the executive producer, and it's my job to get the film made on time, on budget.

O

Becoming a wife and mother and raising a family will always be my number one priority. But I think it's vital to also do things that feed your soul. You cannot give to others without taking time for yourself. It took me thirty-five years to realize that. I gave my all to my work, audiences, friends, family, and bosses, and at the end of the day, had nothing left for me. Once you have children, it's so important to have that next path or direction in your life laid out. If you're not sure what that is, self-reflection is in order. Even with a newborn or small child running around, it's important to take an hour a day for yourself and do what makes you happy. Whether that's taking a bath, going to the salon, shopping, sleeping, anything.

For me it was diving into my creative side, and that's where I am today. I'm putting on paper the ideas that come to my mind that I used to hide away because I was too busy pleasing everyone else, too busy performing to delight an audience. It was almost a relief when I finally began to write. I had ideas for books, documentaries, and scripted television series, and I started to write and write. I just couldn't stop. It was like my fingers couldn't keep up with all the thoughts that were inside my head. While I reclined in my office chair with Gabriel fast asleep on my chest, I wrote about everything and anything, all hours of the night.

I refer to this creative calling as my ninth life, and it would evolve beyond writing. As had happened so many times throughout my journey, an opportunity knocked on my door. I had a friend over for dinner who was working on a movie that she was filming twenty minutes from my home. The coincidence couldn't be ignored. I wanted to create films and television, and here was a production company in my own backyard.

The company was called Brain Power Studio, a media content maker that produces over ten movies per year catered to family audiences, such as Christmas movies and cozy mysteries. I emailed the CEO, Beth Stevenson, and told her about my background. She wrote me back and set a time to meet for a socially distanced coffee date, since the pandemic was still in full swing. I was excited about this meeting, but I really didn't know where it would lead. I never saw myself in front of the camera, but on the production or creative side. However, Beth and I immediately connected, and she quickly became a mentor to me. She offered to review my writing, which I was grateful for.

As we were nearing the end of our meeting, she mentioned that she had a gymnastics script in development. I was obviously intrigued. She explained that it hadn't been produced because the timing wasn't right. Timing is everything. Like me, she felt it was fate that we met, and with my Olympic gymnastics background, I could be an asset in getting the film made. I was excited to read the script and would relay any advice I could.

I read the screenplay, and it resonated with me. How could it not? The main characters were two sisters who had lost their mother at a young age and were raised by their single father. The dad tried his best to give his girls everything they needed, but struggled at times with being alone or having the means to help them be the best gymnasts possible. I immediately thought of my mother and all the hardships she went through to support my gymnastics dream. The script was speaking to my soul, and I knew I needed to be a part of it and help bring it to life.

I submitted my notes, which were well received by Beth and her team. We had a few more calls about the script, and they eventually hired me to executive produce and star in the movie! As an executive producer, I helped with casting and other elements required to get the film to a place that would be authentic to the sport and the young girls and aspiring gymnasts who were the target audience. We integrated some elements of my gymnastics career, including my switch from artistic to rhythmic gymnastics, and how my father used to call me his "little Olympian."

When it came to casting, it was essential for the gymnastics to be as high-level as possible. I had seen other gymnastics movies that made me cringe because the level of gymnastics was so low, and they were not an accurate depiction of the top level of the sport. I wanted to see the faces of the gymnasts as they did leaps and flips and not cut to the landing, knowing that it was a stunt double. The production company shared my vision and wanted to cast top-level gymnasts who knew what it took to have rivalries but maintain a co-operative team spirit and encourage one another through their toughest skills. We also needed star power from the gymnastics world. Two people that came to mind were Nastia Liukin and Chellsie Memmel. I had been on gymnastics tours with them and knew what exceptional gymnasts they were, but I also knew that they were exceptional human beings who continued to motivate young gymnasts.

Nastia Liukin was the 2008 Olympic all-around gold medalist and Chellsie Memmel was a 2005 World Champion and 2008 Olympian as well. Since retiring from gymnastics, Nastia had gone on to host her own competition, the Nastia Liukin Cup. I called her and we spoke about the movie, and she immediately wanted to be a part of it. She felt that the sport needed some positivity, and this was a fantastic way to give back. She was cast as Coach Reka.

Next, I called Chellsie Memmel, who was working very hard to make a comeback in gymnastics. After retiring, continuing to judge and coach, and having two kids, she decided she wasn't done with her gymnastics career. She was training again and inspiring not only young gymnasts, but also older gymnasts who had retired but also had that itch to get back on the beam. Chellsie was creating waves in the gymnastics world, and I knew she would have such a positive impact if she agreed to be in our movie where she would play herself.

Then Beth asked me to play the role of Brianna, a sports commentator. I accepted, but I was very nervous and intimidated because I hadn't done much acting. The kind of acting I did for Cirque du Soleil was with my body and movement, and not using my voice or reciting dialogue. This was a new challenge for me, and as you know from my story, I love a challenge.

Once on set I gave it my all and managed to overcome butterflies and nerves, no doubt helped by my years performing in from of massive audiences, and the small crew was warm and kind to this newbie actor. I performed my lines with confidence and tried to take on my character as best I could. I also went to set on days I wasn't acting to supervise the filming.

My mother was an extra in the film, and if you watch, you'll see her right behind me in many of my scenes. Now that you know the sacrifices my mother made, you understand how special it was to act in my first movie with her. To top it off, we filmed at the very gym where I started doing artistic gymnastics, and where my coach told me to switch to rhythmic. To be where I am today, an Olympian, actress, and movie producer, and be back in my old gym where it all started, went beyond full circle, it was at once bittersweet and mind-boggling.

The title of the movie changed constantly before its release. It went from *Beam Team* to *Little Olympians* to *Young Olympians*, and finally to *Olympians at Heart*. I loved the title and found it to be very fitting. Whether you are an Olympian or not, you can always strive to be an Olympian at heart and give whatever you are doing your all. As we wrapped filming, I was excited and introspective. I couldn't believe that a simple discussion with Beth back in October of 2020 about a family-friendly gymnastics movie had wrapped in April 2021. I was officially an actress and executive producer overnight. My dream of having a creative life was off to an incredible start.

○

I sometimes wonder why I didn't discover this passion to write and create content sooner. However, I stop myself because I know deep down that I needed to live what I lived and experience what I experienced. Good, bad, and challenging moments all led me to this place. I'm not afraid to fail, or not be perfect. What I am afraid of is not living up to my full potential. I want to look back on my life and think, *Wow, I really gave it my best shot.*

One thing I'm good at is perseverance. I don't like to give up. It can be a downfall at times, and isn't always received well, but if you want to get anywhere in life, I believe it's important to fight for what you want and what you believe in. You are your own cheerleader and advocate in life. That's how I want to be remembered, as someone who has helped shape the world for the better and for my kids to be proud of what I accomplished.

Having kids really puts your life into perspective. What will I leave them? Will they be proud of where they came from? I want to motivate my children to push beyond the skies for every dream or goal that they have. It may sound cheesy, but I mean it with all my heart. This one life on earth is short. Live your dreams, shoot for the stars even if no one believes in your passion. No matter how foreign or absurd it may appear to others, you are the only one that can get yourself to the top and be able to stay there.

I've fought this fight many times in my life. I was constantly reinventing myself, and I'm grateful that my mother always taught me the importance of resilience. Now, for a happy ending and a true testament that perseverance and faith will always get you where you need to be, my mom got her fairy tale ending. She met her current husband, Lorne, and lives a beautiful life as a snowbird, with winters in Fort Myers, Florida, and summers in Toronto. She was finally able to retire. Lorne has become a father to me, and I truly thank God every day that he came into my mother's life when he did. He is wise, a gentleman, intelligent, and a true blessing.

My brothers are doing well, too. Mike became a school principal in Toronto and remarried and welcomed a son. He is very happy. Matt, the "man of the house," has a beautiful wife named Cheridan and lives in Europe tending to their business empire. So, while 2012 was our personal *annus horribilis*, we have never been better. Cheers for never giving up and always having faith!

Remember, life will always throw curveballs at you. If you aren't ready to duck and get out of the way, you'll get hurt and become stagnant. My dream for all women reading my story is to motivate them to search deep within and find their passion. No matter what mistakes we have made in the past, they don't define our future. Forgive yourself, forgive others, and forgive the past and move forward. Holding onto guilt or grudges only holds you back from your full potential. Reinvent yourself and your life daily. We are all unique, powerful, and worthy of respect. Never let anyone hold you back. Dive into areas unknown headfirst, pray daily, dream the unimaginable, and set goals for yourself that seem impossible. Nothing is achieved without hard work and passion. I am a true example of this. I've been a child artistic gymnast coached by my father, a rhythmic gymnast, an Olympian, an acrobat, a solo aerialist, a creative director and choreographer, an entertainment executive, a wife and mother, and now a writer, producer, and actor — my nine lives, so far.

## My Three *Rs*

I want to leave you with my theory of the three *Rs*, use them as I did to navigate tough decisions, or to figure out a next step in your life. They apply to virtually any situation.

Ask Yourself the **Reason**.

- What is your reason?
- What helps you get out of bed every day and thrive?

Don't Be Afraid to **Reinvent**.

- When one door closes, break down more doors!
- Thrive on the word "no."
- When one path doesn't fulfill your reason, it is time to reinvent and get moving.

Remember: It's Your Life and Your **Right**.

- You have the right to choose your life.
- You have the right to say no and to stay on *your* path.
- You have the right to reinvent.

O

I hope my story of reinvention and how I came to live "nine lives by thirty-five" will encourage you to dig deep into your own heart. The road ahead will be tough, but don't let anything get in the way of your happiness. Own your life, own your truth, own your strength, and own your talent and your dreams unapologetically. Perhaps your journey will unfold in multiple lives as mine has. Just like the proverb, "A cat has nine lives. For three he plays, for three he strays, and for the last three he stays." And I can say, with my heart full of joy, that I'm staying. Staying present, staying hopeful, and staying thankful for the nine lives that God has granted me thus far, and for the next.

# ACKNOWLEDGEMENTS

When it comes to the writing of this book, I owe many thank-yous. I know there will be some people that I've neglected to mention who were vital to my success and guided me along the path I'm on today. To those not mentioned, I appreciate you, I thank you, and I love you.

To my literary agent, Murray Weiss, who took a chance on a young woman with many lives to summarize in one book. I will always be grateful for your patience, understanding, and help finding a home in this world for my story. You helped make me a better writer and, more importantly, a better person. Thank you for continuing to make my dreams a reality and for connecting me with incredible people that will help and inspire others.

To Kim Izzo, who found the words when I had none, who helped me pull up memories that I didn't know were there anymore, even when the emotions that I felt were unwelcome, and who stood by me in times of doubt or insecurity. You gave me my voice back and helped me move past the trauma and hard times I thought I had overcome. You are not only an incredible talent, but also a true friend, and I know that it was God's will that our paths crossed in this world. Thank you for knowing me better than I knew myself and for shaping this memoir into something that will live on and help my children understand who their mother is and the true meaning of hard work and determination.

To Julie Mannell. In a world full of noes, you gave me the yes I longed for. Our lives mirrored each other's in many ways, and when multiple doors slammed in my face on the journey to getting my story published, yours was the one door that opened. All you need is one person who believes in you, one change-maker that can shape your life. That person was you. Thank you, I will never forget you.

To Olga Filina. From the moment I met you, I knew you had a unicorn talent and calmness that did more than just fine-comb my words. You went above and beyond to peel back the layers of those words and make them jump off the page. Your gift for depth and meaning is powerful, and I'm so grateful that we were paired for my story of many lives.

To Erin Pinksen. Thank you for managing this project from beginning to end so effortlessly. You guided me through every stage of becoming a published author perfectly.

To Kwame Scott Fraser. Thank you for believing that my story can help shape the lives of so many and encourage reinvention through all stages of life. I hope this is the start of publishing more stories of female empowerment and reinvention.

To Karen Alexiou and Laura Boyle. Thank you for taking all my memories and photos and bringing them to life in this book. Thank you for designing a cover that has so much meaning as I hold on to my many lives, mid-leap, with all I have.

To my publicist, Alyssa Boyden. Thank you for taking my story to international heights and inspiring many beyond sport or any one phase of life to continue to challenge themselves and reinvent their lives.

To my boss, friend, and mentor, Robert Herjavec. You took a chance on me when I was a fish out of water in my personal and professional life. I was at a crossroads, not knowing what my life would look like outside of the big stage. As I left my twenties and entered my thirties, you provided me with a once-in-a-lifetime opportunity. An opportunity that, if I worked hard, would allow me to learn any skillset and achieve any dream imaginable. You have taught me to constantly push myself and that I am worthy of success. I've always known hard work is the only path to success, but seeing that unfold literally before my eyes because of your work ethic has been beyond inspiring. You always say, "All the world owes you is an opportunity," and because of those words, I strive to reach the stars with the endless number of opportunities you have given me. You have been a constant male figure and role model in my life, and for that I'm grateful. Thank you for taking a chance and continuously believing in me.

To my dearest Atash. You are the sister I never had, and I just cannot imagine my life without. You encouraged me to fall deep and hard in love when I thought that chapter of my life was over for good. You teach me how to be strong and move past all things with ease. You are my shoulder to cry on and my person when I need to simply dance it out. I'm so grateful to have you by my side in this crazy life. I love you.

To my life coach, Katia. Where do I begin? When we first met, you were a young child reaching only up to my hips, and one of the most naturally talented rhythmic gymnasts I've ever known. Since then you've become one of my best friends, my fashion consultant, my mentor, and my motivator in all things. I'm so grateful to have a friend that pushes me, inspires me, and gives me daily advice. Our whiteboard sessions give me the push I need to make the right decisions and strive to be the best version of myself. Thank you for reminding me to take a moment and celebrate the small wins. Thank you for standing by me and being such a supporter in all my endeavours. I love you.

To my Suzy Q. I've known you since you were a mesmerizing rhythmic gymnast with extreme flexibility and grace, and you're now a dear friend who has taken city after city with me. It's been an honour to witness your elegance in the real world. I admire your work ethic and how you still make time to take such a sincere interest, not only in my life, but in those that matter most to you. You were the only one that came to my tours and are the first to congratulate me and never miss anything. I love you.

To Irina. You were the first friend that I made a leap of faith with, and you reached out to me when I was at my lowest on my mother's couch back in 2012. You were also the one that beat me when I was a junior and then you left the sport for a few months, but always treated me with grace and respect (even when I didn't always show the best sportsmanship or friendship toward you). In all honesty, I envied you and still do. You amaze me. You've been through many hardships, coming to a foreign country and not knowing one word of English, yet your thoughtfulness, generosity, and strength is something I've never witnessed in anyone before. The day you reached out to me in 2012 after years apart changed my life forever and for the better. I will always be grateful to you for that. I love you.

To my Pammer. We reconnected at a time when we needed each other the most. Flash back to over ten years before, when we were competitors on and off the mat. Somehow, in this new life we were united in our need to reinvent ourselves and start over at the same time, again as soloists but off the mat. How we pushed through these times will forever hold a special place in my heart. Life is evolving for us, but our bond will never change. I love you.

ACKNOWLEDGEMENTS

To my Shikha. I'm grateful to you and all our inside jokes. You're the one that makes us laugh when no one else can possibly understand what's so funny. We share a typical gymnast bond, but we share something that is also inexplicable, and you were important in helping me heal and getting off that couch back in 2012. I love you.

To my Emilie. My idol, my friend, my fellow Olympian, someone I call family who helped me navigate so many uncharted waters internationally at a young age. I will forever be grateful to you for taking me under your beautiful swan wing. You never flinched or turned your back on me, you never gave up on me, and you included me in all the beauty that encompassed you. You were my sister on the international stage, and I will never eat a Bounty chocolate bar or a crepe without thinking of you. *Merci mon amie. Je t'aime.*

To the parents that drove me to and from practice, let me sleep at their houses or take power naps before school while my mom worked long hours, thank you. I would not be where I am without you.

To the club owners, managers, coaches, and gymnastics federations, thank you for your flexibility with my family's circumstances. They say it takes an army, and I'm living proof that it truly does.

To my childhood friend, Laura. You were my constant friend outside my gymnastics bubble. You were the "normality" in all my chaos. You reminded me of the faith that grounds me, and to look to God in times of uncertainty. When I ran away to the circus, you were supportive instead of angry that we wouldn't live together and finally be "normal" at university, which was always our plan growing up. You have always shown me support and grace when I haven't always returned those acts of kindness for whatever reason. Thank you for watching me compete at the Olympics in person, and for always taking the time and effort to support me and my dreams. You have always inspired me to be better. I love you.

To my childhood friend, John. You are like another brother to me. You were there as a mentor, not only for my brothers, but also for me. You were a constant for our family in times of turbulence, always there at the drop of a hat. Thank you for rescuing me at the eleventh hour from the embarrassment of attending my prom solo. Instead, you made me look like the cool girl with an older, handsome date! You made the effort to watch me compete on the Olympic stage and cheer from the stands alongside my family, even if it meant sleeping outside on a roof. Through thick and thin, you've been there, not only for my family, but also for me. Thank you.

To Kyle Shewfelt. A fellow Olympian who lit the spark for me to write my memoir. Thank you for believing I had a story to tell. You knew before I did that my story needed to be told.

To Uncle John and Aunt Peggy. You've always kept the spirit of my father alive. You've shown up for every monumental event. You were there when I competed on the world's largest stage and filmed every moment of it so I would never forget it. You paid my mother's way when she didn't have a penny to her name so she wouldn't miss out on the most important moment of my life. I can't thank you enough for filling so much space in our ever-so-small family. You make every occasion a big deal (even if it means attending multiple weddings for the same family members, haha). I love you.

To my brother Mike, a.k.a. Spike. Somehow, we always find ourselves going through similar successes or trials and tribulations at the same time. You were my rock growing up, helping me get good grades and not letting school suffer and hold me back from achieving my Olympic dream. You are my best friend today, and you've been my number one supporter in all my lives and endeavours. You aways made the effort and drove hours on end to see me perform live in Cirque and on my gymnastics tours. Thank you for being my biggest fan. In hindsight, I've always been your biggest fan and admired your intelligence, kindness, willingness to do anything for family, and for simply being the brother I always needed by my side. I love you.

To my brother Matt, a.k.a. Mattycakes. Thank you for being the man of the house. From the moment we lost our father to this day, you've been there for me whenever I needed anything. From unbiased business or personal advice to enhancing my political knowledge (which still needs work), you've continued to make me better. I'm always proud to show you what I'm doing next and to make you proud of me. Your entrepreneurial endeavours inspired me more than you'll ever know. I love you.

To our protector and oldest brother, Mark. You are, and always were, more than a brother to our family. You were our protector, our person to call in times of fear or uncertainty. Throughout your incredible career, which took you to places unknown for months and sometimes years on end, you always found a way to make contact and ensure that we were healthy and safe. I love you, big bro, and thank you for keeping this family safe and secure always, even if from afar.

To my late father, Fred. You gave me my destiny before I was even in this world. Some would say that's a lot of pressure to be born into this world with. However, I wouldn't change a thing. I wonder if you hadn't passed on when you did how things would have played out. I have nightmares about staying as an artistic gymnast and not making the Olympics and disappointing you in the flesh. Perhaps it was all part of God's plan. Maybe, in order for me to achieve the destiny you laid out for me, he needed you to watch from the sidelines, in heaven. God only knows, and one day we will be together and get to reminisce about that Olympic glory I achieved in your honour. I love you and always will, my father, my coach, my inspiration.

To Aunt Corinne and Uncle Marty. You were a second mother and the only father figure I had in my life as a child. Auntie, thank you for being there for us when we had nothing and no sense of direction. Thank you for taking us in as your own children. And thank you for passing down your love of all things, especially clothes and Christmas. Uncle, we share a special bond as musicians and performers. You were someone who knew what it meant to transition from an artist to a traditional career. You always made me feel like I wasn't alone in that transition, and we shared the highs and lows of it all. Thank you as well for those turtle ice cream days when all I needed was a shoulder to cry on between my gruelling training regimens. I love you both dearly.

To my husband, David. Many romances begin when you least expect them and at the worst of times. That was how our story began. Both of us were jaded and untrusting, and I was embarking on the busiest period in my career. Yet somehow, we made it past the turbulence and now have our beautiful children to show for it. I will always be grateful to you for grounding me in a tumultuous time in my life and for your patience as I subconsciously overcame my past. I pray this book will help you understand me even more. Even now, there are still barriers and mountains to cross, yet you stand by me and are my rock, no matter what. I love you.

To my mom, Jaci, and present dad, Lorne. Mom, look how far we've come! We rarely look back, but when we do, it is special. Special to see that even in the lowest times, we were still by each other's sides and would get through whatever was thrown our way. It feels like we're now living in a fairy tale compared to the life we once lived. But that's God's will and his favour, which we often discuss. To my dad, Lorne. Words can't express my gratitude for giving my mom the life she finally deserves, and for breaking the pattern of abuse she once endured. Thank you for giving our family hope and a future of bright horizons. With you in our lives, everything feels whole. I love you both so much.

And finally, the most important thank-you is to God. "'For I know the plans I have for you,' declares the LORD, 'plans to prosper you and not to harm you, plans to give you hope and a future'" (Jeremiah 29:11).

Thank you, God, for the future that looks ever so bright and inspiring, and for continuing to provide a life beyond my expectations. Thank you for forgiving my failures and downfalls and accepting me as your child in all the stages of my life. Thank you for my children, whose lives will be blessed by your outpouring of love and strength. Amen.

# ABOUT THE AUTHOR

Mary Sanders has dual citizenship of the U.S. and Canada. She was a two-time Canadian Champion in rhythmic gymnastics until she made the unimaginable switch to compete for and represent the U.S. to honour her father's legacy. Mary's dad, a Big Ten Champion from the University of Michigan, was a coach and mentor until he passed away from cancer when Mary was eight. To this day, he remains the fuel to her fire. Overcoming an incredible set of challenges from the outset that would have deterred many, she looked to her single mother and older brothers for inspiration. Mary became a 2004 U.S. Olympian in rhythmic gymnastics, two-time U.S. Champion, Pan American Champion with five gold medals, Four Continents Champion, two-time Athlete of the Year, USA Gymnastics Hall of Fame Inductee, and earned the title as the most successful rhythmic gymnast in all the western hemisphere.

Cirque du Soleil scouted Mary immediately following the Olympics in 2004 to perform in two of their touring shows, *Corteo* and *Delirium*. Mary continued her career in Cirque du Soleil for ten years as an acrobat, contortionist, trampolinist, rhythmic gymnast, aerialist, artistic coordinator, choreographer, coach, and creative collaborator in corporate sponsorship.

Mary was hired as the co-creative director, choreographer, and performer for the 2012 and 2016 forty-state Gymnastics Tours of Champions starring Simone Biles, Nastia Liukin, Aly Raisman, Jordyn Wieber, and other members of the U.S. women's Olympic gold medal–winning team. Both tours were the most successful post-Olympic tours in USA Gymnastics history.

Mary has also worked for many years alongside executive producer, *Shark Tank* star, and cybersecurity mogul Robert Herjavec. She runs the Entertainment and Global Partnerships division and directly supports the CEO in all functions.

Mary works in front of the camera and behind the scenes in large productions for TV and film. She is an executive producer, writer, published author, and actress. In her free time, Mary enjoys helping young professionals and athletes transitioning out of sport to find their direction in the next stage of their lives.

Through her memoir and public speaking, Mary is hopeful her story will empower and inspire women of all ages to constantly reinvent themselves in their personal and professional lives.